Deeply We Are One

An Experiential Guide to Recognizing Your Divine Nature and Understanding Your True Connection With Life.

Kate Heartsong

Dedication

To my beloved children Evan and Jamie

and

to Humanity

Table of Contents

Acknowledgments   ix
Introduction   xi
The Interconnectivity of Life   1
Inner Wisdom   7
It's a Matter of Perspective   13
Recognizing the Greatness of Who You Are   15
Have you Become One with Yourself?   19
Exploring Your Personality Traits   23
Techniques to Embrace Your Greatness   27
We Are Creators of Our Lives   33
The Expansiveness of Life   37
Tapping into Your Inner Wisdom   41
Pieces of the Puzzle   45
Distinguishing Between the Soul and the Personality   49
Connectivity of Life and Functionality   53
Getting Back to Center and Being Connected with The One   57
Embracing Your Greatness and the Hologram   61
Mirroring: That which is Inside is Projected Outside   65
More Connections Than Meets the Eye   69
Understanding Your Connection to All Life   71
Recognizing the Interconnectivity of Life Creates
  Positive Outcomes   75
Trust and Surrender   77
The Necessity of the Expansion of Life   81
Emanating The Creator's Qualities and the Light within You   85
Feed Your Life with Thoughts of Plenty   89
How Thoughts Manifest onto the Physical Realm   91
Moments of Despair Can Be Moments of Enlightenment   95
Love Essence   99
Creating an Atmosphere of Courtesy and Respect with Others   105

Trusting and Creating Positive Thoughts   109
Living Authentically   115
The Ripple Effects of Living Authentically   121
Fulfilling Your Life's Purpose   127
Cumulative Experiences of Your Life   131
Creating Peace Within   133
Why Change is Important   137
Bringing Joy and Peace into Your Life   141
Connection with The One and Expansion of Humanity   147
Bringing it all Together   151
Creating a Vessel for Receiving   157
Be an Ambassador   159
We Are All One   163
Appendix A Personality Traits   167
Glossary   169
About The Author   171

Acknowledgments

First and foremost, to Spirit, the Creator of all life. I am so deeply grateful and immensely honored to be the messenger of this material.

I would also like to acknowledge and thank Jerry for his encouragement, dedication, and support; Barbe for her wonderful mentoring; James, Eugene, Tim and Toni for their extensive knowledge and creativity and Karen for her excellent editing expertise.

Introduction

Throughout the ages humanity has always had the capacity to interact in a way that will create peace and harmony. It is essential to bring this forth now for there is much unrest on our planet. In order to create a solid foundation for harmonious and effective human interaction, it is necessary to recognize that we all come from the same source of life. Many know this as God or the creator of all. When we have a better understanding of this, we better appreciate the concept of oneness. It is because of the oneness, and our connection to The Creator, that we are *all* of divine light and goodness.

Part of what this book explains is that the basis by which we can better understand and appreciate the concept of oneness is to get to know ourselves better and through this, gain a better understanding and appreciation of who we are and the absolute magnificence of our being. We will also gain a better understanding of the importance of our individual role here on earth as well as the role that other people have. Through this we will also gain the valuable appreciation and respect for others and for all of life.

There are many words to describe the creator of all life. These words include God, Spirit, The All That Is, Universe, Lord, I Am, The One, The Divine, Allah, Buddha, and others. In order to easily represent the concept of that which has created all of life, in a manner that is all-inclusive, the term The Creator or The One has been used throughout this book. Substitute this with any word that you feel corresponds to your representation of the creator of life. What is important here is the meaning your word has for you personally.

You always have the opportunity to choose what you experience. This is true for your participation with the exercises, tools, and meditations presented here. Know that in order to better understand and experience this book's knowledge, it is important to have a sincere desire and sincere intent to embody and to participate in what is offered. The material is only as effective as to the degree that you choose to participate in. It is, after all, an experiential guide.

This book is not going to be involved so much with the whole subject of thoughts and what they do for your reality; however, it is important to recognize the impact that your thoughts have upon your life. Remember also that intentions with thoughts are quite powerful in the effect they have upon you. You must be clear with your intentions and thoughts about what it is you desire. Also be aware of the intricacies of the knowledge you are reading and how it relates to your life and also in what areas in your life they apply.

There are many approaches to learning what is being taught in this book but these exercises and tools are simple and easy to comprehend, which makes it easier to assimilate the concepts into your body of knowledge. This, in turn, makes it is easier to include the suggested practices into your daily life.

Remember to embrace from this book only that which you feel comfortable with and yet at the same time it is of utmost importance to keep an open mind to the material presented here. For as you allow yourself the privilege to be open to receiving new information you can let this information pass through your filters and see what settles in. You can leave room for consideration of this material in a way that is similar to trying on a new glove: try something new on for size and see how it fits. See how you *feel*. You may be pleasantly surprised by the positive results.

Authors receive information for their books in many ways. In this case, I, as the author, received all of it through divine inspiration, with the material flowing from my spiritual guides. Some people use the term channeling to describe this method. My spiritual guides identify themselves simply as Archangel Michael.

In recognizing The Creator, remember to recognize the divine in you. For you are the light and the representation of this life force. You are magnificent in all ways!

Many blessings of joy, peace, harmony and abundance to each of you as you journey on your path of life.

Peace on earth, goodwill to all,

Kate Heartsong

Chapter 1
The Interconnectivity
of Life

It is important to realize that we are all connected with one another and with all the plants, animals, sea life, minerals, Mother Earth, stars and the whole of the universe.

There are certain criteria that can help establish the understanding within your own life in order to better live in the realization of the interconnectivity of life. You may say having and living this knowing of oneness is a new establishment for mankind. Having this is important because the old ways of living are simply not possible anymore; they do not work. This is evident when you consider that for thousands of years there has been war, yet this has not brought worldwide peace.

It is time to make a change and this change involves understanding the concept of oneness. You can easily understand this concept, and the concept that all of us are connected with each other, when you comprehend that you are a creation of The One, therefore you are part of The One. You and The Creator are one and the same. When you recognize this, you can then better realize that everything and everyone is part of The Creator, and therefore all of us are connected. Remember that The One is all there is and from The One comes everything. There can be no separation when there is only The One. When you understand that we are all one, with each person being a unique individualized part of The Creator, with a specific purpose to fulfill, you can better realize the concept of oneness.

Here's an example: There are many systems that are vital to the functioning of a city. The police that manage the city, trash collectors who clean up, people providing food, teachers teaching, government governing and so on. Take away any one of these functions and you can immediately see that there is a hole, a lack, and a difficulty of continuity. Imagine if trash were not picked up. What discord this would establish in your city! Then once again "restoring wholeness" when the trash collectors come back to pick up the trash. This requirement is the same regarding the planet and the ecosystem. When you take out one thing that may seem small, you actually start to erode the balance and proper functioning of the planet. The interconnectivity of the planet and the smooth operation of living on the planet requires all elements to be in place; every system, every organism, every cell. The entire planet is made up of interconnected microcosms.

Studies show there are symbiotic relationships among all areas of the earth. Once you realize this, you can appreciate there are organisms that will not survive without their host, and the host suffers as well, not having the benefit of the organism. When you apply this notion to the planet and the people on this planet, you will understand that there cannot be an effective symbiotic relationship with Mother Earth and her people without both parties doing what they need to do. You can well imagine that Mother Earth will function fine without the people, for this was the case for many millennia before people came to the earth. But the people cannot live without Mother Earth.

So we are going to establish again the need and also the inherent good to recognize the oneness of all. Remember this includes all people on all corners of the earth regardless of age, race, religion, or background. We are indeed one and the same, coming from The Creator, the one source, which is known to some as God, Spirit, The All That Is, the Universe, the I Am, Buddha, and the many other names representing the originator of all life.

To better understand the connectivity of all of life, it is best to understand and connect within yourself. Once you have established the connectivity to yourself in this manner, you will have a deeper relationship with yourself. It is best to remember that the essence of who you are is indeed connected to The Creator, and this is within you. There is a common perception that there is a separation between the ego and The Creator. Remember that all is connected so even though the ego is seen as being the "separator," this is not quite the case. There is some truth in the ego causing separation, but in the end, what is really the case is the ego is also part of The Creator. It is part of you and therefore it is one with you as well.

It is good to realize the ego can come from a place of separation simply because energies are being fed in such a way as to bring it to a higher light of separation. What is identified as separation is merely a form of energy. It is the nature of this energy to have the requirement of "needing" energy to be fed to it to keep it at a certain energy level. This energy level is different than the energy vibration of your higher source or essence. The separation of the ego is what is perceived, simply because this *is how* it can be perceived in this 3-D world. In fact, there is no separation; it is only the energy form being of a different vibration. That is simply all it is. The essence from which you come from is of the *highest* vibration, and because of this, it is within you at all times. It is there, no matter what other energy influences arise.

Once you establish and understand that the ego is still and always has been one with you, you can relax into the knowing that The Creator is there with you all the time as well. How can it not be? It is always there within your realm because it is all there is. This is also true with the ego. It is there all the time with you because it comes from the same source that everything comes from, The Creator.

Ocean Meditation
Sit with this concept for a few moments now and let the truth of these words settle into your being. Take a few minutes to meditate and assimilate this knowledge. Sitting in your silent

sacred space, allow yourself to breathe and to become aware of your breath. This breath is the breath of life. Being aware of the breath, allow yourself to become even more still within yourself. Be aware of any body sensations you have and be aware of your heartbeat. While you're aware of your heartbeat, see and feel the ocean's waves rise and fall with each breath. As you connect with the ocean's waves, be aware of how it might be if there was no movement of the ocean. The ocean is calm, quiet, and still. While you're imaging this you can then appreciate everything being quiet and still. When you imagine the waves again, know that they are part of the ocean yet are of themselves as well.

Also remember there is life within the ocean. An entire ecosystem of fish, plants and mammals, as well as rocks and sand make up the elements that embody the ocean. If the fish or plants were removed, the ecosystem would be quite different. If the plants were removed, where would they be moved to? Where would you put them? Imagine this in your meditation. Now as you contemplate this, try to imagine how these plants would survive out of their environment. It is analogous to the trash collectors we spoke of earlier, being that when the plants are displaced, it causes a discord in the system Because there is interconnectivity between all elements of life, taking an element out of its place causes discord. Continue to contemplate and be still with this for as long as you desire. When you are ready, come back to the place of conscious awareness and out of meditation. Take another deep breath as a reminder of where you are and a reminder of life.

Now to recognize another aspect of the vastness of life's interconnectivity consider the community where you live. We will again use the analogy of the city, this time looking at the different compartments required to run a city. You will recall that we discussed the vital role each segment plays in the smooth operation of a city. Consider the microcosmic work and details required to run a company. This company provides the utilities to the city. There are many facets to this. The maintenance people repairing the electrical systems and

grids, the workers installing new service for a home, the sales representatives, the managers, the installers installing the new equipment
for a new grid of electrical power, the billing department, the collec-
tions of these bills, the power generator that creates the electricity,
the gas piped in, and the process for finding, obtaining and purchas-
ing this gas.

This is quite an array of functions that are involved with operat-
ing just one large company. Certainly it reflects the necessity to have
proper communication within each department, and proper effective
communication between many of the departments in order to have
the successful outcome: proper service for the customers. Imagine
if just one area did not work properly, for example, the piping of the
natural gas not coming in as expected. Imagine the havoc this would
create. The emphasis of the company would be to expend much more
energy in their activities to repair this disconnect. In the meantime, a
ripple effect occurs in other departments; for example, the customer
service representatives are affected by the larger volume of calls received from disgruntled customers and the billing department can't
collect because customers are not getting what they want so they
won't pay. This in turn will affect the amount of revenue coming into
the company; therefore, there will be fewer resources for them to pay
for the natural gas that they need to buy. You can see from this single
example how many departments are affected by just one event.

Let us now expand this idea to the economy of a nation. When
there is one area that is not properly functioning, it has a ripple effect upon most or all of the people. Let us look at the economy of the
United States. When billions of dollars are being given out to the war
in Iraq, millions of people in the United States are left with fewer resources (less natural gas). It has a huge impact on the day-to-day lives
of the American people by not having the resources available to run
a nation smoothly.

This large-scale impact has an effect on smaller elements as
well; namely, people. People's emotions are strained and there may be

fear of not having enough of life's basic comforts. The body's reaction to this is stress; and stress will create a multitude of negative effects on the physical body and on the emotions, as well as the spiritual and mental aspects. So you can go from the macro—the nation—to the micro—the human body. There are many parallels to these systems. It is vital to the human body to run smoothly to optimize energy and vitality, joy, and productivity. When the body is compromised, as in the case with stress, the systems do not function in an optimal manner and there can be symptoms manifested in the physical body. This in turn may create less productivity, less joy, less harmony with one's self and with others, and more worry and more illness.

The universe's energetic system further demonstrates the concept of interconnectivity. Each person has an aura, which is the universal life force that is connected and unique to each person. There are also auras on plants, animals and the mineral kingdoms. Beyond this is the ether, or unseen energy, that interconnects everything. You can recognize this by remembering the way you felt when the phone rang and you thought it may be your mother, and it was! You may have had a feeling that something was wrong with a loved one, only to later learn that your loved one just found out she has an illness. When you are at a party and suddenly get the urge to turn your head toward a certain direction, you notice someone is staring at you. You have picked up on and felt energetically that person's presence focused on you.

By examining these examples of interconnectivity, you can have a better appreciation that everything in life is connected, has its place and that each system is important. There is a vast interconnection within all things, all the way from the macro level to the micro level.

Chapter 2
Inner Wisdom

This is a gift from the great Holy Spirit.

Throughout the ages certain people had information flow through them. They were called prophets. Today the term is channelers. You can well imagine that the soothsayers of biblical times were also in the position to give advice to the kings and queens who sought their attention and advice. The same is true today with the astrologers, mediums and psychics.

It is time to realize the depth of the information that is available to you in the form of The One. This is known as inner wisdom. The truth is always within you. This is all encompassing and all prevailing. Once you can grasp this, then you can be aware of this information at anytime.

Come explore a passage of time that will help you understand one way inner wisdom was used. The Babylonians used their inner wisdom to explore new country. They would meticulously examine an area with great insight and connect to the land they were considering exploring. They used their inner wisdom to be aware of the nuances and subtleties of the areas and plots of land. Soon it would become apparent that they would find the land they sought. Their connectivity to explore and seek answers came from their inner wisdom. This is still found in many of the indigenous people around the world. There is an understanding among these people of all life interconnecting and an appreciation and reverence toward all, including Mother Earth. There is a symbiosis between these people and Mother

Earth, so much so that there is difficulty among them to distinguish between themselves and the earth. They have an appreciation of the natural forces of life and nature.

As has been for many years and is currently the case, western culture does not possess the understanding or awareness that we are intricately connected to nature and to all of life. There continues to be a disassociation of the human spirit from the land. Reverence for life has greatly diminished and people often feel very separate from others, from the natural elements of the earth and even from one's self. It is as if there is only a small capsule running around, trying to bring itself life from within its own ecosystem when in fact this ecosystem expands largely all around, but the person is unaware of this. There may also be an unawareness of how he affects himself, others and Mother Earth. There is much need for awareness and knowing that there *is* interconnectivity. There is a need for understanding the interwoven intricacies of all life.

When we can consider the notion that there is but one creator that holds everything together and that in fact all is created from one source, The One, then we can begin to understand how all is connected.

Tapping into our Inner Wisdom
Coming to the place of innermost wisdom and having accessibility to this requires many thought processes be undone and unlearned. Part of the journey of this section is to describe the techniques you can take to come to a place of revealing what has always been within you and within each one of us. The innermost sanctuary of life, the life force essence, The Creator, resides within you. These processes are easy once you apply yourself with a sincere intention and desire to bring change into your world. You will be delighted to have access to this new area of your being. It has always been there for you, and now you have a greater ability to reach it, to know it, and to tap into its wisdom, which is really *your* wisdom.

Begin by intending to think from the heart. Be of light heart. Be of the knowing that this can indeed be a possibility for you, that you can and will access your inner wisdom and reach a new and a higher ground of consciousness.

Exercise
Start now by simply being aware of the environment that surrounds you and also of the environment called you; meaning, be aware of your body and your body sensations. Practice today to simply be aware of the people you meet or see, the activities you perform, your mood, the traffic, the environment, animals you encounter, and all the intricacies of life. Be aware as well on how you affect others and the environment. And most importantly, be aware of your thoughts and judgments as you observe the surroundings you find yourself in. Be aware, but don't criticize yourself for your thoughts or judgments. Simply be aware. Also be aware of your awareness.

Beneath everything lies the current of the ever-flowing stream of life, which is known as The Creator. In the capacity of this flow, you will learn to dance and sing because you are within the realm of The Creator. Once you have been accustomed to the flow in this new living arena, you will be amazed at the expansiveness that flows from within you. The higher realm of existence (The Creator) will relay the information to each one who decides to tap into this vast knowledge.

You can open to a whole vast world of intelligence and knowing, simply by being in tune with yourself, accessing your inner wisdom and setting the intent to do so.

Techniques for Tapping into Your Inner Wisdom
We are continually being asked to assess the many choices we are given each day. Sometimes there are hundreds of choices to be made during the course of just one day. No wonder we are thinking so much! When is there time to have the silence to listen—to listen to that small quiet voice of our inner wisdom, our inner guidance? This

is why meditation and quiet activities, such as walking in nature, drawing, painting, martial arts, and any other activity that forces us to be in the moment, the now, are so vital to our well-being and are excellent techniques to accessing our inner wisdom. When we can establish this type of practice on a daily basis, giving it sufficient time to work, then we can be better equipped to hear our inner guidance during the course of our everyday lives.

Here are some pointers that will assist you in helping to establish meditation as a daily routine:

- Set up a designated time each day to have quiet time.

- Dedicate at least 15 minutes each day to this. Of course, longer periods of time are more beneficial.

- Set a special place to practice your mediation, although it can certainly be done anywhere, but having it in the same place daily helps deepen the experience faster than it would otherwise.

- Incorporate an ending to your meditation to bring closure. You may want to do this in any number of ways. Some suggestions are to end it with Amen, Namaste, I am with The One, This is done, or And so it is. Another option to close the meditation is to visualize a special symbol that is dear to you.

- Some meditation practices become rote. You become so accustomed to them that they don't create the same stimulation they once did because you have acclimated to them. It is highly recommended that different meditations and exercises be practiced and that you switch from one to another from time to time. This way, you don't fall into the same place energetically.

Remember there are also other types of quiet time you can create for yourself, such as walking or creating artwork that will assist you in listening to your inner wisdom. Try those techniques that suit you best. As with anything else, it takes practice and dedication.

Living in the present moment, the now, is another way of accessing your inner wisdom and living in connection with your divine nature. This is the point in which you are focused only in the present and not thinking of the past or the future. When you are totally in present time, you are more keenly aware and more connected. This then allows for easier access to your inner wisdom.

In addition to meditation and living in the present moment, the following are techniques you can incorporate into your daily life that will assist you in living more consciously and be more aware of yourself, and this in turn helps access your inner wisdom.

- Set an intention for the day. This takes place in the quiet time of waking up and is a powerful way to start the day. As you wake, establish your intention of the day. It may be to have a joyous day or to accomplish certain tasks or to simply wake up being refreshed and ready to take on whatever is given to you. This setting the tone for the day is most powerful because it is within the realm of being between the sleep state and wake state. It is when the veil of life is thinner and so the intention is more powerful. The veil is a metaphor to describe the separation from The One that we perceive ourselves as having.

- Upon laying down to sleeping at night, give thanks for your joyous day, or your achievements that day and set a prayer of intention for your sleep, such as sleeping soundly, remembering your dreams, or solving a particular issue in your life. Anything you so desire to set your intention on will become more potent when you are in these relaxed states of mind.

- When you embrace the loving person that you are, and realize the grand magnificence of that which you really are, this facilitates being more positively aware of yourself and living in connection with your divine nature. There is nothing wrong with thinking highly of yourself. Quite the contrary, it is necessary to embrace the gloriousness of who you are. Why do we know this is true? Because you are created from the source of all life, The One. When you embrace this within yourself, you can more easily embrace this in others. That is, you can more easily see the grand glory of *each* person on earth. This also helps facilitate your knowing of the interconnectivity of all life. When there is this knowing of the divine within each person, you can then more easily embrace and live the path of the most high, The One.

You can understand and appreciate the great divinity that resides within yourself, and all others, by recognizing each one of us has a gift or gifts to express. You can appreciate and see the wonder of the uniqueness of each and every person. Even if they have difficulties, even if they are of a sound mind, even if they are handicapped (in your judgment of it), even if they cannot speak, even if they are in prison, even if they are an infant or of old age, no matter what person you see, there is always the same divine connection within them as there is within you. How can it not be? You all come from the same source. When you recognize the reality of The One, you recognize the reality of all life, plants, animals, minerals, humanity—all of the universe.

Chapter 3
It's a Matter of Perspective

There is nothing that does not come from the same source.

Which is the Whole?

When we consider there are many varieties of life, and there are many potentials for life within the vastness of this planet, we must simply ask where did this all come from? Who would be responsible for this? How can there be such variety, yet all be here on this planet called Earth? There is a commonality among all and this is the groundwork that makes it easier for us to begin to understand there must be something that holds the variety of life together. Certainly the laws of physics and gravity are partly to explain, but there are also many unseen laws.

We can see the greater part of the earth from a satellite or space shuttle, but what we are seeing is the grand scale of it. From this perspective, we cannot see the individual components of the earth; we can only see the wholeness, which is from a macrocosmic perspective. By physically being on this earth, we can see from a microcosmic perspective. This allows us to see the individual plant that is on the piece of ground we stand upon. Which is the whole? The earth we saw from the satellite, or the piece of ground we are standing on? If we were to ask an insect what the insect's world is comprised of, it would say the whole is the area where he lives, but if we were to ask the astronaut he would say the planet is the whole. Both of course are correct; it is simply a matter of perspective.

The Consciousness Vantage Point

Let us carry this knowing into the next concept that will help us understand the interconnectivity of all life, the consciousness vantage

Kate Heartsong

point. We are seeing with a limited perspective, which to us is our whole perspective, but from the vantage point of the higher realms of consciousness, it is only a part. If we were to expand our awareness to the higher realms of what we know as The One, then we could see the whole perspective and therefore have access to all the knowing and information there is in this realm. Wouldn't it be nice to have a pathway or avenue by which we could access all this information easily, so that we may have the same vantage point the astronaut has from the shuttle looking upon the earth? Meditation and living in the present moment are two effective pathways that help us create this ability. With sincere desire and intent, it is possible to do so.

Chapter 4
Recognizing the Greatness of Who You Are

How do you come to have the deep knowing that you are connected to The Creator? You can begin each day by appreciating and respecting yourself.

If the reality of The Creator can become part of your everyday existence, if you are able to fully incorporate it within yourself in a sincere way, if you can comprehend the notion that you are indeed a part of The Creator, then you can fully embrace this to the point of full expression of who you are. You can begin each day with a prayer of sincere gratitude and acceptance that you are indeed of The One, knowing deeply within yourself that this is true.

Think of how the body functions, with several systems within the body's system. When you consider the enormity of this, it is astounding. Also consider that, in conjunction with the body, you have your mind (your thinking capacity). Think about it. What really is entailed with thinking? What does it involve? Where do thoughts come from? Where do they go? Then, add to this the coordination of these two systems (the body and the mind) in conjunction with emotions. Yes, emotions are a separate function from thinking yet they occur at the same time that you are thinking and at the same time you are functioning with your body.

No wonder you can think of yourself as all powerful, all mighty, and connected with The Creator. How could you think this is nothing less than a miracle? How could you doubt that there is indeed a greater Being that has put this all together—this thing called life?

Looking at the miracle of life, we can then begin to deeply appreciate the functions occurring on our planet, our dear Mother Earth, which houses so many life forms. Expanding the concept of the three systems just described, to the realm of Mother Earth, we can see there are many activities happening simultaneously with her as well. How can we explain that? And how can we begin to understand that there are so many variations of life on Mother Earth, each seemingly with their individual capacity to live? Yet, no life form can live in isolation; each requires food to keep it alive. There is a relationship between the animal and its food. There is also the relationship between the water and the plants, the plants and the air, and the air and the ocean's life. There are so many arenas that show the intricacies and the interconnectivity of life.

Now imagine again what we just described on Mother Earth and expand this to the concept of the interconnectivity of the planets within the solar system. Each, with their own unique gravitational pull is in some way interdependent upon the other planets. Yes, this concept extends to beyond the planets themselves, to the sun. The sun is also interdependent upon the galaxies, each one having a certain gravitational pull, as well as the requirement of energies expanding within them, all helping to further the energies of the sun itself.

Each galaxy is interdependent upon other galaxies. These concepts can become difficult to fathom, but nonetheless, the parallel concepts all remain the same—there is the necessary interconnectivity within *all* systems, anywhere from the smallest of creatures to the largest of galaxies, and beyond.

So why is this being discussed? What purpose does it serve us to understand the intricacies and interdependence upon other things? It reminds us of the vital importance to recognize and embrace, live and deeply know that we are part of this interconnectivity. When we can come to grips with the notion that we are indeed of The One, that we are ourselves The One (in an individual form), then we can once again become more in tune with our truest essence. When we achieve this, we have indeed come into our own power and true embracement of who we really are.

Reminders of Your Greatness

Here are some easy and readily available tools that can help you become more in tune with the greatness of who you really are. It is important to set an intention as you practice these.

- Each day before rising, while in between wake and sleep, remind yourself of the wonder of the earth and all of its glory, and visualize yourself in this space of the glory of The Creator. You may want to picture yourself in a beautiful garden, or in a favorite place that brings you utmost joy. Place yourself in this atmosphere and sense and feel yourself there. Do this for a few minutes until you start to actually feel the emotion of joy. Be with this for a few minutes, the longer the better, although even as few as five minutes will be beneficial.

- Wear a piece of clothing that you are truly comfortable in, or an item that makes you feel special. It can be as simple as a pin or hat or it can be an outfit that you love. Wear this item as often as you can.

- Take a special bath from time to time to feel your glory. This is no ordinary bath however. Listen to music that brings you great pleasure and enjoy, to the fullest, the sensations of the water against your body, feeling the bubbles running softly and slowly down your skin. Make this a "meditation in the water" bath.

- Be in the presence of The One. You can always bring yourself to the awareness of this presence by being totally in the present moment, and setting the intent to be in the space with The Creator. This will always help you to be in the deepest part of your soul. It helps to center you and to connect you with the divine presence like no other activity, in a short time.

The tools listed here are just a few you can begin to incorporate into your daily life. There are other techniques described in Chapter Seven that will also assist you in bringing you to a place of knowing and feeling your glory. You can even make up your own. Have fun creating a process or technique that you enjoy and that brings you to the place of center, which is connectivity, to The Creator.

Chapter 5
Have you Become One with Yourself?

It is imperative to know that in order to have an appreciation of the connection and oneness of all in the world that you must begin with yourself.

How can you know of something outside of yourself if it's not first a part of yourself? Let us explore the following example: Suppose you come to a river and you want to jump in. You know you can do this, but it may not be wise to do so because there are various factors to consider. How fast is the river flowing? Do you really want to get wet? Can you swim? So, in order for you to decide to jump in or not, you ask yourself these questions. The same is true with knowing of the world. Consider the world your river. How can you jump into the world without knowing certain answers to questions such as who am I as I relate to others? How can I best be of service to others in the world? What can I do to be the very best of who I am?

In order to answer these questions it is important that you first understand who you are in relation to yourself. It is as if you cannot explore the outside world sufficiently without first being in tune with and knowledgeable with your inside world—yourself. Certainly you can go out to the world and interact, and this is true for many people, but in order to do so in a mindful and optimally meaningful way, you must know who you are.

Exercise
Whether in the context of your job, your business, or your daily activities, you can only best offer service to others when you know what your gifts and talents are. You know it is easier to do

what you enjoy than it is to apply yourself in areas that you are not as gifted in. Certainly it is possible, but it does not optimize your joy of life. How do you know you are doing what you love to do? You know this when you have great enthusiasm and joy, and it is as if there is no time because you are in the moment and you are intricately involved with (at one with) what you are doing. Think of a time where you were involved with an activity that brought you utmost joy and happiness. Think of what it was you were doing. Take a piece of paper and list the gifts you have that enabled you to enjoy this activity. What elements about you are unique or special?

Now list other gifts that you have, that bring you joy. It may be as simple as having a green thumb that produces a bountiful garden, or the gift of making others feel special or the gift of "talking" to animals. Or you may have leadership skills that help bring stability to your department, provide loving care for your children or provide companionship for the elderly.

Appreciate Yourself

With the same paper, ask yourself how you feel regarding your gifts. For example, if you have a special gift of helping others by visiting the elderly woman in your neighborhood who doesn't have family here, how does it make you feel when you visit her? What is it about your gift that you can be proud of? What pleasure or comfort do you see that this brings to the elderly women?

Just sit with this for a while and focus on your heart space and intend to feel the warmth here. Ask yourself how you feel when using your gift. Feel the warmth of your heart extend out and now focus on loving and appreciating yourself for having this gift and for sharing it. There is much to love and appreciate here. Extend this warm feeling throughout your whole body and continue to love and appreciate yourself for your gifts for as long as you would like. Repeat this exercise with each one of your gifts and allow yourself to feel self-love and self-appreciation.

Enhancing Your Self-Love

Take a deep breath and breathe in all the appreciation and love you have for yourself. Be aware that it is *essential* that you allow yourself to feel self-love and self-appreciation. You are an amazing, terrific, loving and wonderful person, always and in all ways. The conditioning that you may have received in the past, or the actions that may have been shown to you might make you feel unworthy, but you are extraordinary beyond comprehension, beyond anything else on the planet. It is up to you to regain your self-worth and self-love. You have the power to do this. It is obtainable if you so desire and if you follow the exercises in this book. You are about to embark on the most extraordinary journey of the soul, one in which will bring lightness to your heart and laughter to your soul if you so choose. Be mindful of what is being written here. It is necessary for you to realize that it is possible for you to enhance your self-love and self-appreciation. It is all up to you. You and only you have the ability to think your thoughts.

Exercise
To demonstrate this most simple but profound awareness, sit quietly and notice your thoughts. You are the only one in your head. There is no one else around to give you a thought, and you are choosing to have that thought right now. Now imagine having a thought that brings you joy. Think of another thought that brings you joy. Certainly by reading this book, you are being given instructions to have certain thoughts; however, note that it is your choice to have that thought or not. Sit with this concept for a while. Be open to understand this concept. Be of an open mind to accept this as truth. Through this exercise, you can better appreciate the concept that it is indeed your choice, always, to have a thought or not.

So now that you have a better understanding of this concept, we can go on to the next premise: Revealing yourself to yourself and thus to the world outside of yourself.

Exercise
It is important now to bring yourself to an awareness of your body. Be aware of how you feel this very moment. What change, if any, do you feel in your body? Do you feel warm? Do you feel air against your skin? What emotions are you having now? Where in your body are these emotions? Are you feeling happy, anxious, relaxed or confused? Being in tune with your body helps you become even more aware of yourself. It is also helpful to be in tune with your emotions, the gifts you share with others and the environment. It seems a lot to be aware of at one time, but with practice, it does come easier. And the introduction to this concept will help you warm up to embracing this as a part of your daily life.

Take another deep breath, being quite aware of it, and acknowledge your willingness to partake in the exercise you just did. It takes courage and clarity to be aware of the gifts that you offer to others, to the world, and to yourself.

All Systems Need to Be There
Recall from the utility company example that it is necessary for all systems to be in place to enable the whole, larger system, to operate in full capacity and in an optimal way. This concept also applies to you. Your unique gifts and combinations of those gifts are essential to the whole of life on this planet. It is important to have you. Yes, you. You are unique and your uniqueness is essential to the planet. Sit with this concept for a while, and let it soak into your every cell and into the very aspect of your being.

Chapter 6
Exploring Your Personality Traits

To accomplish your life's goals, you must get to know yourself.

In order to create more joy and to easily accomplish your life's goal, it is beneficial and imperative that you live in connection with your truth, which means to be in connection with the person who you really are. In the exercise in the preceding chapter, you experienced a simple process to identify some of your gifts, which gave you a partial way to discover who you are. We will now explore ways you can discover or affirm who you are in the area of personality. We are going to find some simple ways to explore these inner aspects of yourself, and in doing so, you will get to know yourself better.

Exercise
On a piece of paper, write down your personality traits. This can include having a sense of humor, being friendly, having a strong analytical mind, being artistic, adventuresome or contemplative. Include any negative personality traits as well. You can also reference Appendix A for a list of personality traits.

List these in order of domination, starting with your stronger personality traits. Then examine this list and carefully put thought into each one, getting to know these aspects about yourself. Have an appreciation of these traits and contemplate them for a while. You may discover that you have a larger array of traits then you initially came up with. Now sit with these traits and simply embrace them. Be with them and own them, which means to totally embrace and acknowledge them as being part of who you are. It is important to own all your traits, even those you may consider negative. For in owning, acknowledging and appreciating *all* aspects of yourself, you can better embrace and love the whole of who you are.

If you are having difficulty acknowledging or owning your personality traits, then go back to the previous section and continue to spend time on building your self-esteem and your self-worth. Come to realize the greatness of who you are by reminding yourself many times a day. Allow time to assimilate and incorporate fully into every aspect of your being the true knowing of the greatness of who you are. Allow this to be and it will indeed come forth.

The key to this is to have faith, knowing deep within yourself that perhaps what you're reading may really in fact be true! You have established fully within yourself what you believe to be the absolute truth about who you are. If this is not a happy, bright picture of yourself, if you think negatively about yourself and criticize yourself, then this is all the more essential for you to work on and bring forth into your consciousness the real possibility that you are great, loving, and lovable. You must dispel any notion of self-worthlessness by working with these exercises and by applying the concepts daily with sincere intent and desire. It is vital that you come to a place of accepting that the possibility is just as true, and in fact, is *more* true, that you *are* wonderful, loving and lovable. Embracing this will bring you to a greater understanding of who you really are.

Meditation for Feeling Your Greatness
As explained earlier, you can rest in knowing that there are many ways to bring yourself to a true understanding of the magnificence of who you are and that it is important that you set an intention to do so. The following meditation will help you experience this. Before you do this, though, the concept of a sanctuary will be explained. A sanctuary is a place that is dearly held in your heart as a place of utmost comfort, peace, joy, and harmony. This imaginary place is invoked at anytime you desire and is commonly incorporated into a meditation. This place helps you to more deeply connect to The One and

with yourself. Any and all components of this special place is created and imagined in any way you feel will invoke that sense of comfort, peace, joy and harmony.

Imagine now what elements you would like in your sanctuary. Think of a beautiful area in nature you have deeply enjoyed or use your imagination to create the scenery you desire. Add components that elicit using your five senses, such as hearing a waterfall or birds, seeing beautiful flowers or mountains, smelling the scents of the beach, the feeling of sand in your toes and the warmth of the sun on your skin, tasting a refreshing drink or favorite food. Have fun decorating your sanctuary. You may want to sit in a special chair or throne (remember, you are magnificent, and a throne is rightfully yours). Just sit with this scenery you have created. Feel your comfort and peace as you relax here. Breathe all this in, knowing it is your special sanctuary. You can always add or change this in any way you like. You will return to this sanctuary many times during the course of the book's exercises and you will carry this special place with you in your heart every day.

Continue being in your sanctuary and intend now to go into meditation. While there, imagine having the life of your dreams, with all the material objects and survival essentials that are important to you, as well as much love and joy, and that you're surrounded by the people (and/or animals) that are most dear to you. Imagine how you love and honor yourself and how you see yourself from a perspective of greatness. Imagine also how happy and comforted you are in the fact that all your needs are met. Just feel and be with this now for as long as you'd like. Focus on your heart space as you are imagining these feelings and feel the love within grow. Feel yourself being in the place of the utmost glory of joy and that you allow yourself to feel this joy with great gratitude. Being in this space will help to dissolve the discomforts of what your present reality may be like, if that present reality is not all that you so desire it to be. Taking a deep breath, allow this breath to take you even deeper to this most precious place of sanctity. Allow yourself to be totally immersed in this space.

Now consider the possibility that you really can have what you imagined to have in the meditation just described. What if you took this feeling with you everywhere you go? You can begin to appreciate the enormous benefit of feeling better just imagining this in your life.

Chapter 7
Techniques to Embrace Your Greatness

Start each day by being appreciative of your gifts and talents.

When you come to appreciate the fullness of your liveliness, when you can fully embrace the essence of who you are, when you can completely envelope your capacity of wholeness, knowing so completely your greatness because you are of The Creator, then you can be in a more complete peaceful and joyful existence. If you can remind yourself and remember this every day, it will become easier to incorporate these thoughts into your being and your body's cellular memory.

There are techniques you can incorporate into your daily life that will help you become more at ease with yourself. Pick and choose two or three, or more, and be consistent using them. You will see marvelous results as a result of incorporating these into your daily life.

• Be mindful of how you speak to yourself. In what way do you praise yourself? Criticize yourself? When you do something wrong are you being kind and understanding as you would a child who innocently makes an error? Or are you the critical parent who is admonishing the child for the behavior? Think of how you would want to be treated and spoken to. How would you speak to a friend for having made a mistake? You would probably be compassionate and understanding because we are human and after all, sometimes things happen. Be mindful to become your own best friend in this regard. Be kind and understanding that you made the error. Learn from it and move on.

- Talk with yourself as if you were The One. For in fact you are the creator of your life, co-creating with The Creator. How respectful are you toward The Creator? How reverent are you with regard to all of life? When will you recognize the divinity of your being and hold it up high as you rightly should? When you can hold yourself in high esteem and know it is not from ego, then you can more fully embrace the great, extraordinary, and unique person that you are.

- Sit in stillness and contemplate your accomplishments of the day. Get a journal to represent the grand accomplishments of your day, perhaps one with an exquisite or special design on it. These accomplishments are called grand, but this does not mean they are necessarily of a grand magnitude. What is meant is that everything you do is a grand accomplishment, no matter how small. For example, picking up your child from the daycare can be considered an accomplishment. Why? Because you are being reliable and dependable in your capacity of motherhood or fatherhood by showing up for your child. This is a grand accomplishment. An accomplishment can also be delivering a great speech to an organization you belong to, because you are sharing information with others that can benefit their lives, if they so choose to apply it. Preparing a meal is a grand accomplishment by bringing nutrients to you and your family's bodies. Think of all the things that you do each day. All of this is considered grand.

What about the accomplishments of the mind? Consider when you are consoling another human being with your kind words. When you solve a math problem for your college entrance exam and feel good about it, you have used your mind to accomplish this task. When you consider the many decisions you are confronted with each day, deciding what to buy at the grocery store, where to turn while driving to a friend's, what to wear, etc., you are accomplishing great things with your mind.

The same can be said with your emotions. You accomplish more when you are happy and less when you are sad. When you make the concerted effort to be happier, you have accomplished a great thing. You have made yourself feel better.

We can consider accomplishments in the capacity of the spiritual realm as well. When you pray with sincerity for the healing of a friend, you are accomplishing a great deed of sending caring and loving thoughts. When you meditate, you are accomplishing a greater balance and peace of mind for yourself and you are also helping the people of the earth through this practice.

As you can see, your accomplishments are endless. Now write down twenty accomplishments you have done today. You will be surprised and amazed at what you have accomplished.

• Find the little things in life that have gone right for you and recognize your blessings. There are many things that you don't even have to put your mind to that just happen automatically. Your breathing, for example, the breath of life. We are given the gift of breathing and we don't have to think about doing it. Other examples of what your body does automatically is walking, talking, and moving about. Your organs know exactly what to do in order to function properly without any thought or command from you.

What about your car starting in the morning, the stove turning on, the coffee pot working, the water running? All these things that we take for granted can easily be seen as simple gifts of life. Step back and assess what is in your life that can be appreciated and not taken for granted.

Now list twenty things you can appreciate that went right for you today. Really sit and contemplate this concept. The simplicity of this can bring a deeper sense of gratitude in your life. This can help you feel better about your life, even if you are experiencing great difficulties right now. When you can view your life as having many blessings, you are creating a better avenue of receiving more joy and greater good into your life.

It is important to use these techniques on a regular basis. It will benefit you to incorporate these exercises into your daily life. For example, you may want to start out your day writing five things you appreciate: a roof over your head, a warm bed to sleep in, a hot shower, food in the refrigerator, your health, the fact that you woke up. Then, as you go to bed, write down five things you accomplished that day and five things you are grateful for. This is an excellent way to remind you of the many accomplishments and blessings that are in your life. It doesn't need to take more than two or three minutes, but the results, and the benefits, will be long lasting.

- Prepare something special for yourself on a daily or weekly basis. These can include such things as taking a special bath, preparing a special meal, reading a good book, taking the time to walk in nature, buying a special cup of cappuccino, making a phone call to a friend, bringing yourself a flower, getting a massage or pedicure. Choose something that you may not necessarily do on an everyday basis, but something that has the essence of being special. The important thing to remember is when you are doing this for yourself, do it in a manner that exemplifies the greatness of who you are. Think of it as giving yourself a gift; how would you do this if you were doing it for a special friend? Do it for yourself in the same manner. Make it exciting, sacred, loving and kind. Putting the essence of love and caring into it will greatly exemplify making it special and thus give it a special meaning.

One Positive Act Leads to Another

The kindness that you bestow upon yourself is beneficial for you as well as for the world. For when you are being kind to yourself and are treating yourself as special, you then feel better about yourself. When you feel better about yourself, you are happier. When you are happier you are kinder and more helpful to others. Imagine a world in which people are appreciative and happy. There would be a greater tendency to be more helpful and more respectful toward others. We would truly have a more loving and peaceful world. So you see, as you are being kind and loving to yourself, as you are seeing the greatness of who you are, you are helping the people on this great Mother Earth. And this is where we can better appreciate the oneness of all life. The connection within ourselves and to ourselves has an effect on the connection to other people, to our immediate surroundings, immediate family, friends and co-workers, and also an effect on the whole planet by means of the connecting source that binds all of us together, that being The One.

Remember, it is up to you to choose to make a positive change in your life. Incorporating these steps into your day-to-day life will help you reach your goal of being happy and at peace.

Chapter 8
We Are Creators
of Our Lives

All your intentions and desires can come to fruition when you believe that you can do it.

You must embrace the knowingness that you have the ability to create what you desire. On the other hand, when you are in a place of complacency, there is no forward movement in your life. It feels as if you are stuck in a holding pattern and out of alignment. What brought you to this place? What can you do to change this place of loneliness and isolation you may have within yourself?

Inner resources

There are places within that can bring you comfort. The key is to tap into the vastness of all that you are, which is *always* within your reach. It is who you are, and the depths of this are within you, part of you, on you, around you, and through you. Tapping into this place of inner abundance is simply connecting deeply to yourself, finding a source of comfort and calm within, rather than seeking to find comfort outside of yourself.

Certainly it is important to know there are outside resources available to you, such as a close friend, who can bring you comfort, but it is important that you know you can tap into your own resources for it is within you at all times thus it is always available to you. When you use this wellspring of inner abundance, you can more easily make available to yourself the resources of creativity, which means you can depend on your inner strength of belief to tap into this source so that you can create what you desire. With the appropriate intentions and desires, and the ingredient called belief, you can co-create anything you want. It is a matter of delving into your inner resources, your wellspring, that provides the foundation of courage and faith, the foundation of strength for your resilience to carry forth your intentions and desires.

You can further develop this ability to access your inner wellspring by knowing and believing that you are fully capable of creating. This type of belief strengthens your ability to co-create.

You have the ability to reach and tap into these abundant wellsprings of comfort and of positive energy at any time, whenever you so choose. It is a matter of remembering and choosing to do so. For when you decide this is where you want to be, then you can bring forth the abundance of life and vitality back into your life. It is a matter of choice. This point cannot be overemphasized. It is essential to understand that you have the choice at every moment of your life. What can you do to tap into this inner abundance? You can begin by saying these words "I am willing. I choose to believe I can indeed tap into my inner abundance of my life."

Believing is important. Remember the words of Jesus: "It is done unto you as you believe." It is not the other way around. That which you believe comes forth because this sets you up for your ability to create.

Meditation to Remember Who You Are
Find your favorite chair or sofa to sit in and get comfortable and begin with a simple but powerful meditation that will help you remember the creator that you are. This will help you believe that you can tap into the deep inner realms of who you are, your inner abundance, and from here you will then discover how to be more in tune with yourself and more in tune with the interconnectivity of all. Begin with the usual centering and once you are in your place of connection, say and repeat the fol-

lowing words "I am a connected child of The Creator who has a life of great abundance and ease. I believe in the creative abilities I have and from here can choose to go anywhere I want."

Sit with these words and contemplate them. Know and feel what these words represent. Words are simply a way to express an action that is to take place. While still meditating, set the intent to go even deeper still by simply repeating this to yourself and you will arrive into a deeper place of connectivity. When you do, you will feel even more peaceful and in more connection with The One, and with yourself, which is one and the same. Stay here for as long as you care to and when you're ready, come back and open your eyes. You are the creator, co-creating with The Creator. It is helpful to realize that you can come to this place at any time to gain insight or answers to a particular question.

Chapter 9
The Expansiveness of Life

Everything is connected, from the farthest reaches of the galaxies all the way to our individual cells.

You can sense the wonder and expansiveness of The Creator and also realize The Creator is within you by being still and being aware. Try this now with the following meditation.

The Stars and Cells Meditation
Bring yourself to that quiet place within, setting your intention to open your heart space. Imagine being in a very special place, such as your sanctuary. Now as you imagine yourself here, become aware of your breathing. Remember that this breath of life comes to you and for you. Let yourself align with it by allowing yourself to *feel* your breath. Imagine the stars in the heavens so far away, as you breathe in. Then imagine your individual cells as you breathe out. Again, imagine the stars as you breathe in, and your cells as you breathe out. Keep feeling this awareness as you imagine the stars and cells. Stay with this for a few minutes.

Now imagine a certain time in your life that brought you great joy. This could be the birth of your child, your wedding day, the graduation or birthday celebration of a loved one, or any other event that brings you joy. Now, continue with your thoughts on this celebratory event, all the while still continuing with your awareness and feeling of your breathing. Imagine bringing this feeling of joy and celebration into your very being, into the very essence of who you are. Be with this for a while, embracing and absorbing this experience. Become aware of how you feel now. Is it a feeling of joy, peace and/or excitement? Take a deep breath and allow every fiber of your being to be interpenetrated with this sense of aliveness.

Now become aware of the vastness of all life by reflecting on the stars you imagined. With the same sense of joy and celebration that you are experiencing, imagine bringing this out to the stars. Sit with this for a while and be with the expansiveness of this feeling. You can better appreciate the connectivity of all through this experience. You can also better know the oneness of all life and the magnitude of The One being with you and you being with The One. Can you feel this expansiveness and the extraordinary wonderment of life?

You can choose to bring on and invoke this feeling at any time by setting an anchor now. An anchor is simply a stimulus or reminder that, when you think of it, will bring on the feeling that was associated with it when creating the anchor itself. Set an intention to simply remember the scene you placed yourself in at the beginning of this meditation, and feel it, breathe it, believe it. Now create a visual stimulus, such as the scene or visualization you just used, and breathe this in. Intend that this stimulus is now anchored in you and that you can bring up this feeling when you think of the vision that you just anchored. Be still and absorb the feeling for a few minutes and allow yourself to become totally one with it.

Gently bring yourself back to your present environment.

The Forest and Trees

The experience you just had will give you a sense of the oneness of all life. You can understand this by imagining a forest, which, as you know, comprises a large area. Now focus on just one tree. By doing this, you are experiencing the oneness of that tree. Now imagine climbing to the very top of this one tree and looking out to see the whole forest. You would see all the trees working together to make the whole. Seeing and experiencing the whole gives you the feeling of the expansiveness, and seeing and experiencing the individual tree

38

gives you a sense of the one tree (yourself). Recognize that without the one individual tree, there could be no forest. All the trees work together to become the forest.

You can expand this concept by bringing your awareness to the ground upon which the tree sits. The individual insect that lives at the base of this tree has its whole world in that area. To the insect, this area is its whole world. To us, it is a microcosm; to the insect it is a macrocosm. This is simply a matter of perspective. See with new eyes as you walk about in your daily activities at the vastness of life, the expansiveness of all, the variety of life that is here with us, the variety of people and the combinations of personality traits within each person. Recognizing the expansiveness and variety of all this will help you appreciate the enormous expansiveness of The Creator. The richness of life and the variety of life is so compelling to see, that you can have a deeper awareness of the interconnectivity of all of life.

Systems within Systems

There is also a great vastness of the inner world of your physical body, and the molecular level of life. Take, for example, the extraordinary process of transferring blood throughout your body. This requires the integration of bringing nutrients into the blood stream, the pumping mechanism of the heart, the proper balance of nutrients that enable the molecular structure to disseminate the nutrients, the proper balance of oxygen to help bring the nutrients to where they are targeted to go, and the ability of the cell wall lining of the arteries to receive the nutrients. All these processes take place without you consciously trying to make it happen, yet it does so with great efficiency (so long as you have the proper elements in place). Given the fact that these processes happen for your body, it is vital to recognize that when these individual processes work together, they form a whole integrated system. If you were to take apart the processes that are required to perform this function of providing the body with the proper nutrition and fuel to live, the function cannot occur. Therefore, it is imperative that *all* the processes are in place, with the proper balance of each, to work efficiently together to provide the goals of providing proper nutrition and energy to the body.

So you can see how there is interconnectivity of the processes within your body, just as there is the interconnectivity of life on the planet and the expansiveness of the stars, planets and solar systems. There is both macrocosm and microcosm, depending on your perspective.

You can expand this concept even more by exploring the details of an individual cell. All the components that are necessary for the proper functioning of an individual cell are also required for it to work in harmony with the other cells to perform its overall function. For example, the cells making up the liver, the cells making up the blood stream, or the cells making up the skin, all function in a similar manner, yet they serve different functions. And all are essential for the functioning of your whole body, as well as for the functioning of each individual cell: Systems within systems.

There are also systems within an individual cell, and between each cell. Looking at even smaller parts, we see there are components within an atom, each working together to properly function. When you get further into the space within the space, you can see an expansiveness just as you can see the expansiveness of the stars and solar systems. It is, once again, a matter of perspective. You've seen what is required in the functioning of a human cell, a human organ, a human body, a human environment, a city, a state, a continent, the earth as a whole, the solar system in which you live in, the galaxy and the other stars and solar systems that exist. You probably now have a better appreciation for the infinite expansiveness of The One.

Chapter 10
Tapping into Your Inner Wisdom

Since all is connected, we have access to all.

The truth of the ages is that you are indeed connected with The Creator, and therefore are connected with others. Since The Creator is all there is, and has and continues to create everything in the universe, you can see there are connections and interconnections within and of all things: people, places, animals, plants, minerals, the Mother Earth, solar systems, and so on.

Now you can continue to explore the realms of the inner world, your inner wisdom. Imagine there is an infinite network of information that can be accessed once you know how. The key to doing this is to believe you can and also to be in harmony with The One, which is the interconnectivity of all. For when you recognize the interconnectivity of all, and recognize you are part of that connection, you can better appreciate that you too are part of the intelligence of The One and tap into the rich knowledge that is there for you.

How can you tap into this knowledge? You begin by simply being aware; aware of your inner body and your inner connection. There are several ways to do this. By daily meditation and prayer, by contemplative times of quiet to "hear" the inner wisdom, by observing yourself, and by being in tune with, and really present with, yourself and with the people you are with.

When you tap into and access all the knowledge waiting for you, you are better able to live your life from a place of interconnectivity, you are better able to make decisions based on your inner wisdom rather than from the head and intellect, and you are better able to interact with others on the planet. Something else to be aware of is that it is vital that you communicate from the heart, live from the heart, and make decisions from the heart.

Meditation to Receive Inner Guidance

Have your pencil ready and write down the information you are about to receive through your inner wisdom. You will go into quiet meditation and contemplate the very essence of your being, The Creator within you.

Get into your quiet place, into your sacred space of solitude and meditation. Remember to focus on your heart space by closing your eyes and looking toward your heart. This helps you focus on the heart space. Also, set a sincere intent to receive any inner wisdom that is there for you to receive at this time.

Now, inhale a deep breath and exhale while examining the different aspects of yourself, thinking of your gifts, your talents, the special uniqueness you offer the world. Feel the warmth of your heart as it expands. Feel it envelope your entire body, all the while paying attention to your breathing. Sit quietly for a few minutes in this contemplation and see yourself in your sanctuary. Bring with you the elements of who you are. As you are in this sacred still place, allow your mind to quiet and ask for any inner wisdom and guidance that The Creator has for you. Simply sit in quiet and allow yourself to hear any words, feel any feelings or see any images that may come forth. Be relaxed with this process, truly believing that what is happening is happening perfectly. Write down any information you receive without editing it, writing down whatever comes to mind. Continue with this until you feel the process is complete.

Now bring yourself back to the present environment, open your eyes and breathe in the inner wisdom/guidance you received.

In case you do not feel you have received any information, know this is perfectly acceptable. Also know that sometimes information will come to you after the meditation. Simply practice this meditation again and soon you will be able to receive the inner wisdom. Remember to set a sincere intent for success, truly believing it is possible. Everyone has this ability. Like any muscle that hasn't been used regularly, with practice and patience, you will get better at this.

Chapter 11
Pieces of the Puzzle

It is of the greatest treasure to be upholding The One in our hearts, for when we do, we can best celebrate life!

It is always of the grandest nature to be connected to The One. We see, for example, in the animal kingdom a connection to The One by the synchronicity of the birds flying together. How are they to know what direction to fly in unison? They are in connection with the oneness of life, their symbiotic unison with their lives, in the air flying and having pleasure in the mere act of flying. We see a similar connection with the fish in the ocean. They are also in unison, swimming together as they do in a natural flow and rhythm of life. They gather together and become one with the movement and become one together. Consider their whole pattern as being one. You can see this as well with the trees and the connection they have with one another. There is an orchestration of beauty among all the trees that comprise the one forest. When you see all these trees combined to make the whole forest you will see the majestic beauty of The Creator. When you travel to the corners of the earth you may see many things that remind you of the magnificent wonder of all. There are so many areas of life that have a great bounty of goodness coming forth.

There is within each life form an energy—a life force that wants to, and cannot help but, come forth. The energy life force that is unique to an oak tree is the same life force that causes the bumblebee to come into existence. It is the same life force that causes the oceans to flourish with massive variety of life forms, each having its unique features, yet doing what all life forms do and that is simply to flourish and grow into what it is meant to grow into. The human form is no different. It is here to flourish and bring into the world the unique gifts and talents that it was designed to be that is so vital to the planet.

You may wonder, how can someone who is homeless contribute to the whole of the planet? How is it that a poor African child, who cannot find enough food to live on, flourish? How are these people contributing to the whole of the planet?

To understand the answers to these questions, we must come to understand there are many unseen forces that contribute to the whole. We in our humanness, can only see and know to a small extent what really is happening. But to really comprehend why each individual person, animal or plant contributes to the whole, we have to realize this understanding only comes from the perspective of The Creator, the great connector of all life. Human life has only a few pieces of a puzzle, and therefore, cannot see the whole picture, simply because, by its very nature, it just doesn't have all the puzzle pieces required to see the whole. On the other hand, it is The Creator that has all the puzzle pieces and therefore sees and knows the whole picture. We are of a limited perspective; The Creator sees the whole perspective.

Exercise
Come to a place within yourself now to imagine looking at all of life. This can include anything that your mind first thinks of, such as butterflies, the ocean, mountain peaks, or whatever you imagine. See in your mind the many wonderful life forms. Now just sit with this for a moment, and mentally picture the different life forms. Now imagine you are on top of the highest mountain peak. From here, look around. What can you see? You will probably see other mountains and clouds and some undistinguished scenery in the distance. You do not see any specific life forms yet you know they are there. You are seeing from the perspective of The Creator, in which you see and know the wholeness of all life. Now, as you go down the mountain, you encounter other human beings. You are now recognizing these specific life forms for the uniqueness of who they are

and the great capacity of their lives. By seeing the individual person from the perspective of The Creator, you can appreciate who they are. And you know that they can become what they are to become, flourishing as they do because they are putting forth their unique gifts and talents. We may not know from our human perspective what their unique gifts and talents are, but from the perspective of The One, who has all the pieces of the puzzle, this full understanding and knowing exists.

Chapter 12
Distinguishing Between the Soul and the Personality

There is a strong foundation, an inner well of strength and fortitude, which always resides within you and you can access this at any time.

You can begin each day knowing that all is well and for your highest good. It is as if it has been created in advance. Yet you also know you have free will. This is where you can begin to see the distinction between your soul and the ego. The ego serves to function by giving you a specific identity, known as the personality, separate from other humans.

Remember the personality, which comprises many different combinations of traits and characterizations, is simply that which distinguishes one person from another. It is where you live from in your daily life. It is the outer shell of your being. While your personality must be available for daily activities, it is the orchestration of The One that helps to define the ongoing purpose and divine reason for you being here in this lifetime.

The soul is the connector to The One and provides the deep nourishment that guides you on the path you are intended to live. It is your soul that is that portion of your being that guides you when you listen to it. Other words for the soul are higher self, inner guidance, gut feeling and intuition. When you listen to your inner guidance you are better able to carry forth your life's purpose and are better able to live joyfully.

The Timeless Nature of the Soul

To help demonstrate the distinction between the personality and the soul, consider a tree being analogous to the soul and the leaves of the tree being analogous to the personality. The tree is always there; solid, ongoing, and stable. Imagine the tree has budding leaves, ready to come forth. You can imagine the excitement of the upcoming renewal of this aspect of the tree. Continuing to grow, the buds get bigger and turn into leaves, until the leaves completely develop. Then, during the course of the spring and summer, the leaves thrive, soaking in the nourishment of the sun, the photosynthesis needed for the well-being of the tree as a whole. You can see in the fall the leaves change color and then finally fall off. The cycle renews and starts over in the spring but first of course is the inner quiet and rest during winter. The tree is still there, it still exists, yes, but there is the quiet and inward existence that defines this part of the tree's life cycle.

When you can compare this analogy to the cycle of a human being you can begin to understand the interconnectivity of the "seasons" of a person's life and the seasons of the tree. The tree is analogous to the soul, which is the foundation; it is vast and deep and is always there, having strength and stability. The leaves are analogous to the personality, and just as the leaves change from season to season, the outer aspect of your life (your personality) changes over the course of your lifetime.

When you compare the tree's cycle to your human life, you can see that your life comes forth in newness as does the tree's buds, and over your lifetime changes in your personality reflect your cumulative experiences and personal growth, as do the emerging leaves and their growth. And there are times in your life when you have a quiet time, like the winter of the tree's life, in which you rejuvenate, hibernate and restructure. You can also be aware of the ongoing foundation of self, which is your soul (the tree) and recognize that it is always there. The timeless nature of the soul has the instinctual knowing of what to do, how to go forth with its natural cycle, and what to do next in order to live its life purpose, which is to be just what it is supposed to be—a tree—or in your case—you. Your soul level is that aspect of you that orchestrates your being so it will always lead you to do what you are meant to do, which is to be who you are, bringing forth your talents and unique gifts to the world.

So you see in this analogy of the tree and your soul that they both orchestrate the life of the entity they are supporting. It is best when you are aware and are listening to your inner guidance (soul), for when you do, you live your life as it is intended, which is simply being who you are.

Chapter 13
Connectivity of Life and Functionality

There is an interconnectivity of functions that bring together all of the whole, together forming The One.

When we recognize the bountiful abundance of the earth, when we really appreciate the wonder of nature, when we have a reverence for life, when we completely respect ourselves and others, when we comprehend the wholeness and unity of all, then we will have a better understanding of the most highest will of The Creator, which is complete acceptance of what is, so we may go forth unencumbered and have a joyful life! Live in joy and harmony within ourselves, share and be this with others and come to a place of reverence for all of life in *any* form.

Functionality

Perhaps you now have a better understanding for the unity of all life and how all of life is connected. Understanding this connection is vital to the positive outcome of our species. When you have this knowing, there is no need for competitiveness or angst and no need to try to get something from someone, for when you're in a place of joy and harmony, you realize there is enough abundance to go around. You can better appreciate the giving and receiving, which is an exchange of energy. You can be free to share what is yours, or at least what you've identified as yours because in the ultimate reality, nothing is really "yours," for all is of The One, of the continuous flow of all life. It is merely broken into segments for the purpose of easily identifying what goes where. It is as if the sacrifice of separation is such that it enables separate functions or purposes, so that the whole of life functions as it should. You recognize the need for separating the things you identify as your own simply because it is a way for you to then begin to apply the notion of functionality.

For example, say you are a firefighter. You function as and live your life in this capacity and thereby extol your individual identification. To do this, you live in your own ecosystem, while being a part of the macrocosm of the city you live in, which in turn is part of the state you reside in and the country you reside in and universe you reside in.

Living in the ecosystem that enables you to function as a firefighter, you bring together the elements of what you need for yourself to flourish. All of this leads to identifying yourself as a firefighter and brings forth the attributes that go along with the ability to do this function and fulfill this purpose.

You can appreciate the concept here that nothing really "belongs" to anyone when you simply see that all things come from the one source and are simply parceled out to serve and help bring forth the functionality of a person's gifts, talents and purpose that he or she is here to fulfill. All of us need to have our basic needs met (food, shelter, love) so we can better serve our function and purpose. We also have certain talents to carry that function and purpose out into the world, and need certain material objects to create the comfort and ability to fulfill our function and purpose.

We are better able to accept the truth of the unity of life when we realize our own oneness and connectivity to all of life. When we recognize it within ourselves, we are able to recognize and appreciate this oneness within another.

The ability to attain a reverence for all of life is better when it comes from within first, for what is within is what can then be brought forth. We cannot give what we don't have, so let us turn to what we can do for ourselves to better cultivate the sense of knowing the oneness within ourselves.

Meditating is an important practice to experience oneness within yourself. When you devotedly meditate on a regular basis, you are more easily attuned to your inner source, your inner strength, and can access the vastness of The One, which is really yourself, since we are all one connected. You can more easily access this domain of silence by setting an intention to quiet your mind. How do you accomplish this in your busy life? You do so with a sincere desire to have this consecrated time for yourself.

When you practice presence within yourself you can better practice presence with others as well. You create the sacred space of connectivity and total focus with another in the same way you connect with yourself, for it is within these sacred spaces where The One exists. So whether you are in the domain of silence within yourself or in connection with another, you are—when focused and fully present—in the sacred space of The One, the absolute reality. You can better understand this when you realize your connectivity to all life. Your consecration is such that when you delve within, you can better hear the heartbeat of the one life. And when you can better hear the oneness of all life, you resonate into the vibration of The One. In resonating with this space, you are able to reside in this space of connectivity with The One in your awakened state (not sleeping or meditating) for longer periods of time.

Deep Meditation
Begin with a simple meditation that will strengthen your ability to go deep within and accentuate your knowing of the oneness. Close your eyes and take a deep breath. Imagine being in your beautiful sanctuary. As you focus intently on your breathing, say to yourself: "It is I who have come to myself and I intend to go deeper still into the vastness of my true being."

Say these words with deep desire and intent. Feel these words sincerely with great pride knowing that it is indeed possible. It may help to come up with an image that helps you feel as if you're going deeper into your own self. Perhaps you'd like to envision being a deep sea diver, going deeper into the depths of the ocean and as you go deeper, you go deeper within yourself. Or perhaps you'd like to feel the glow within your heart that continues to expand as you go deeper. When you feel this expansiveness, you also feel the connectivity and oneness of all. It may be as if you can no longer feel your physical body yet you know you are still here and are safe.

Once you are feeling this deep space of oneness, also be aware of your energetic body. Your energetic body is simply that aspect of yourself that is not physical. How does it feel? Do you feel light? Thin? Do you no longer have a sense of your physical body, but feel the expansiveness of it, yet a sense of nothingness, at the same time? You may experience feeling peace, calm, joy, and a sense of well-being. Simply observe yourself in this space with no judgment.

Be aware of your thoughts, and let them gently leave, without condemning yourself for having thoughts. Also, be aware of the silence between the thoughts, holding onto these spaces of silence to hear Mother Earth's heartbeat. Become aware of your heartbeat. No judgment, simply awareness.

Reside here for as long as you would like to continuing to feel your space of peace and joy, the place where you feel safe and connected. When you are ready, gently bring yourself back to the present environment.

Chapter 14
Getting Back to Center and Being Connected with The One

It's up to you to choose to live or not live in the realm of The Creator.

Using a memory from the past that solicits great joy and peace is a wonderful way to bring yourself into the place of being connected (centered) within yourself and within The One. When you realize you can think about the memory and therefore begin to feel joy and peace, from a past memory, you can better appreciate and know that thinking this type of thought can be experienced at any time you choose. Remember, it's all about what thoughts you choose to have. You can allow yourself the discipline to bring yourself back to center and connection to The Creator when you catch yourself with thoughts of past or future, or with unpleasant or negative thoughts. You can intentionally bring yourself back to the present moment, and be aware of what you are doing in the now, and you can think positive thoughts. Remember, the veil does not need to be there if you so choose. You can go about your daily functions, such as performing your job, going to your school, taking care of your children, but doing so from the place of connectivity to The One and connectivity to all life forms.

So how can we accomplish this? You can bring yourself back to center easier when you are in a constant state of awareness and are in the present moment. Here are some additional suggestions to help you:

- Put up notes to remind yourself to get back to living in the present moment.

- Choose a certain sight and/or sound that you consistently see or hear that is a stimulus to remind you.

- Place a picture or some words that have a particular significance to you in a prominent place that will remind you to go back to center.

- Use something that is unique to you that will be helpful to get back to this most exquisite place from which to live.

    When you are centered and connected you will feel a sense of calm and peace, joy, clarity and mental alertness. It is a state of mind desired by most to be in at all times.
    In addition to the above suggestions, here are some practices for you to incorporate:

- Practice a meditation of your choice once or twice a day. This meditation should bring your focus and awareness deeply into the present moment, with all distractions put aside. As was mentioned earlier, it is best to find a place where you can meditate that is in the same location each day, to build an easier way of prompting yourself into meditation.

- Remind yourself daily of the connectivity of all life. When you go about your daily life, as you observe others, nature, animals and plants, say to yourself: "I see the wonder and marvel of The Creator. We all are created from the same source." As you say these words, *feel* them as well. Be with yourself in utmost awareness while saying these words, or words of your choice with similar meaning.

- Place your attention in the present moment, in the way that you would when you are in a place of joyful concentration. When you are in a place of joyful concentration, you are then able to focus on the task you are performing, whether it is of a creative nature or interacting with someone or working at your job or being in nature.

Exercise

Try this exercise now to demonstrate what we mean by joyful concentration and focused attention. Get out a pen and paper and begin to write down the plan you have for today or tomorrow and as you do, be mindful and focused on the actual writing. Take your time, write slowly and witness the words coming forth from your pen and onto the paper. Witness and observe yourself as being the writing instrument and be aware of the consciousness (yours) behind the writer. Be in complete observation of what you are doing and once you are in this state, consciously have the thought of putting in a feeling of appreciation for your ability to do this simple task. Be totally focused on the task of writing down your goals for the day.

As you continue to write be aware of the feeling and mood you are now in. It is probably one of calm and joy. It may be a feeling of silence and peace.

Perhaps you have a task on this list that is something you don't want to do but must be done anyway. Even though you may not feel good about what you need to do, the exercise you just did probably brought you to the most present moment and thus can demonstrate how being in the present moment brings you to a place of joyful concentration, making the task less difficult to tackle. Access your anchor so you can be in a better place of reconnection. You may recall that when you think of your anchor (the visual reminder that will assist in invoking a feeling), and with sincere intention to invoke your state of centeredness and connectivity, you can bring yourself back to this place of calm and peace.

Remember when you can visualize and think of a joyful experience, you will "go there" with the feelings of joy, as if you are actually experiencing it. Your brain does not distinguish between what is really happening versus what you think is happening. Therefore, invoking a joyful thought will provide the same benefit as actually doing it.

These suggestions are made because of the importance of feeling good and feeling connected and centered with The One. As you recall, it is vital to be in this place of connectivity for as much of your waking state as possible. This will help bring joyful fluidity into your life. And you will then easily bring forth more joy and peace to your day-to-day existence.

It is easy, as we go about our lives, to disconnect from our place of connectivity to The One, therefore it is beneficial for us to remember to practice and incorporate into our daily lives some or all of these suggestions so we may easily bring ourselves back to center in order to feel our connection with The One and feel our connection with all of life.

Remember that the essence of The One is your essence, for you have come from this. This is your source of your life and the source of *all* life.

Chapter 15
Embracing Your Greatness and the Hologram

When you cherish and hold yourself in the same light as The One does, then you have become all the more a master of yourself.

Who can best recognize the greatness of yourself and completely embrace yourself, better than your own self? For who can become more of who you are than yourself? You must come to fully embrace and love yourself to the deepest depth of your being so you can fully embrace The One. For, to know yourself is to know The One. To know The One is to know yourself. Think about this concept. Absorb these words of truth. When you consider the realms within yourself that stand for the goodness of humanity, you can better appreciate The One. Why? What do you think the answer could be? Go within yourself and find the direction or the lead that can bring back to you the answer to this. Begin by examining your own thoughts. What comes up for you when you compare yourself to The One, or when you contemplate the idea that you and The Creator are one? If you agree with this idea, why? If you don't agree that you and The Creator are one, why not?

What can you do to deeply know that you are to cherish yourself, and that The Creator cherishes you? Why, if you don't agree with this, do you feel otherwise? Has it been your negative self-talk? Has your upbringing caused you to think of yourself as less than you really are? It is simply up to you to decide to make a switch to having more positive self-talk and having a more positive self-image.

Kate Heartsong

Exercise
Begin by writing down warm, loving thoughts about yourself on a piece of paper and read it to yourself often or you can write the following down on a piece of paper and read it often: "I am the exact reflection of The Creator, within which comes the whole and the perfection of The Creator, who always provides for all of creation, for when The One creates, it comes from The One Itself. Therefore I am a part of The One, the great creator. For when the tree bears fruit, it is of the tree, simply an individual segment of the tree. In the same way, I am the fruit of the tree. The Creator is the tree and I am a result of it. So I embrace this knowing with all my heart, my soul and my might. With these words I fully embrace The One, and I embrace and cherish myself. It is within me to recognize the being of who I am that allows me to then go forth into the epitome of myself."

The Hologram

Another way to recognize the greatness of who we are and that we are an expression of The One, is to consider the concept of the hologram. When cut into pieces, the hologram is still whole in the sense that all the pieces have the same picture; the same essence of all is still there. The pieces are simply smaller than the original. It is the same for humans. We are the individual pieces of the whole, The One. And we have unique talents and gifts that come forth to be used for the whole of humanity. When we come together in groups, we still represent the whole. Whatever the function may be, there is a tendency to have those of similar purpose congregate toward each other, like a particular segment of the whole hologram (before it was cut into pieces). Together, these functions tie into each other to form larger conglomerates. Recognize that these pieces are still holding the aspect of The One. It is as if The One is interwoven throughout each piece (human), with each piece having its own unique contribution that is vital to the whole. It is the interconnectivity that, by its very nature, holds all together to form The One. We know that The Creator is the vehicle by which The Creator expresses through Its own self, which is expressed and continues to be expressed, through what we perceive to be individual pieces of the hologram. So we can then better appreciate why we are so holy, for we are indeed The One expressing, in the form of our unique self.

Hologram Meditation

Contemplate and meditate on the hologram as being whole and as being many individual pieces and why meditating on this assists you in recognizing the grand nature of who you are. Use your imagination and explore. It is very beneficial and provides for a deeper embracement of the "Oneness" concept, and of the concept of why you are so great, grand, and glorious. Be with this and absorb the absolute truth of who you are.

Chapter 16
Mirroring: That Which is Inside is Projected Outside

When we can begin to understand the divine truth, we can begin to understand that we are the ones we have been waiting for.

When you begin to become within your own being, appreciating yourself, and your gifts and talents, you can then better appreciate others. That which you have within yourself is shared with others. You also see in others what is inside of you. The ability to see what is outside of you, what your outside reality looks like to you, is merely a physical law.

Exercise
You can complete this knowing by trying the following. When you are in a room full of other people, come to a place of quiet and rest, perhaps in a corner of the room. As you stand there, observe your feelings. Are you peaceful, joyful, or anxious? Be in this space simply observing yourself. Then once you have a good sense of where you are with your state of being, start observing others in the room. Simply observe others without judgment. As you observe people, what are their emotions and their state of being? Who is experiencing what you perceive as a similar, or same state of being as you? What you'll likely discover is the people at this gathering, those that come into your focus of attention, will be those who have a similar state of being as you. Why? Because you're already oriented in that state of being so you're more aligned to seeing this in others.

This is called mirroring, or outpicturing. This means that what you see outside of yourself is simply a mirror to what is inside of you. There is a field of potentiality that always exists. The field of potentiality is simply The Creator in the unmanifested form; that is, it has not yet manifested into a physical form. While you and others are in the manifested realm of existence (i.e., physical form), everything else that is not yet created in physical form (manifested) is still in the unmanifested state (the state known as the field of potentiality); that is, it has the potential to become manifested.

As you have thoughts and feelings, and when the same thoughts and feelings occur consistently, the energies of these are signaled out to the unmanifested field of potentiality, and in perfect timing, the thing that was thought and felt comes into form. That is, it comes into manifestation. This is the reflection of what was inside of you, coming outside into your view of your reality. It is a projection, or mirror, of your inner thoughts and feelings.

This process or mechanism by which we manifest is an excellent way to understand the concept of mirroring, where what manifests for us is a result of what we thought of many times (which is coming from within us). That which is within us gets projected to the outside of us and is outpictured (mirrored); that is, it is reflecting what is inside of us.

Understanding this assists us in understanding that we create our reality through our thoughts and feelings. It is important to realize that it takes having many thoughts consistently done over a long period of time to have these thoughts become manifested (come into the physical realm of existence), so having just a thought and feeling here and there will not create it into the physical/manifested realm.

Exercise
Sit and contemplate these words to have a better understanding of it. You can more easily recognize that you create your own reality through your thoughts by doing an experiment. When

you focus on something, you may notice that it gets bigger. If you're feeling sad and you continue to feed this emotion you will feel more sadness. Likewise, if you are at peace and you feed that emotion, you become more peaceful.

The same is true with what you focus on regarding people. When you focus on the positive traits they exhibit, you see them as having these positive attributes, and likewise, if you focus on their negative traits, you will see more negative attributes in them. Remember the sayings "birds of a feather flock together" and "like attracts like"? We are drawn to people who are like us (mirroring who we are). Those around us are a result of our energetic pull. We are drawn to them as they are drawn to us. In the same manner, we see circumstances and material objects of our lives come together as a result of our thoughts. For example, if we are fearful of not being able to get a job, the energetic message to the field of potentiality (The One) is that we are not getting a job, and therefore we see the outpicturing (mirroring) as being unemployed. On the other side of the coin, if we have thoughts of having a wonderful and well-paying job and we know and feel this, then the job comes into existence to us; it is energetically pulled toward us.

Be mindful of your thoughts, the feelings you have with these thoughts and your feelings about these thoughts. They are powerful.

Chapter 17
More Connections Than Meets the Eye

The interconnections of life include the energies of the earth, sun and moon, the universal life force (chi), as well as the people, plants, animals and mineral kingdoms.

Let us explore some of the ways you can more deeply appreciate yourself and your connection to all of life; connections that are perhaps more than meets the eye. One of the ways you can better understand your connectivity with all of life is by looking at yourself and your relationship with the rhythms of the earth. You get up at the dawn of a new day to the sun rising. You go to bed after the sun sets, while experiencing the quieting of the earth.

The cycles of the seasons also represent the cycles of your life. You rejuvenate and regenerate during winter, so you may come out and start anew in the spring, paralleling what the plants and trees do. You are in full swing with your life and activities in the summer and you harvest what you have learned and experienced in the fall. The cycle of life continues.

Your rhythms also coincide with the cycles of the moon. There are rhythms and energies of the moon's electromagnetic field that influence you. When you see the phases of the moon, from your perspective, it appears whole at times and then wanes as the month progresses. Of course the moon is always whole; it's simply your perception from earth's vantage point.

You have a relationship with the plant and animal kingdoms as well. Pets demonstrate this connectivity of life. Pets often know the energies of the planet and the seasons long before you do. The 2007 tsunami demonstrates this. People in the regions where the tsunami hit were not aware of the impending danger but the animal kingdom knew well in advance and migrated to higher ground.

Your association with your pets demonstrates an almost symbiotic relationship. Your pets depend on you and you depend on your pets for their companionship and find great relaxation in their presence. It is as if they can bring The One's presence to you and know of the oneness and connectivity of life.

And of course, there is a connectivity existing between the plants and the earth, the plants and the animals, and the plants and you. There is a connection that exists within you and the universe that amounts to energies and bio-frequencies that must come forth in order for life itself to exist. This is what many know as chi, the life force of the universe. It allows for the energies of life to flow. It nourishes your essence and very being. This chi is of the greatest interconnectivity and most widespread because it is chi that bridges between the unseen and seen, between the unmanifested (pure potentiality) and the manifested (physical form). It is chi that brings life to life.

Chapter 18
Understanding Your Connection to All Life

We are in the midst of a great shift, the likes of which have not occurred in many millennia.

The Creator asks us to be within and access our own likeness, which is of The One. By what means can we examine our association with what we call our own life? How can we better delve into the deep recesses of our souls to establish a better understanding of our connectivity to The One and to ourselves, to the community, to the planet, and, for that matter, to the universe? The answer is through a deeper association with our selves. This is the fulcrum, the focal point, the seat. It is from here that we are better anchored in, and consequently, we are better able to associate and see the relation we have to The Creator and to all that is. For without an accurate, intricate, pure understanding and a knowing of ourselves, it is less likely we can see our place in the whole, and we are thus less able to relate to The Creator and to all that is.

A Walk through a Forest

This might be easier to understand if you can imagine walking through a forest. Unless you know where you're going and know how to navigate, you may have a difficult time getting out of the forest, for there may not be any signposts to show you the way. You may enjoy the journey, but after awhile you may become lost and then worry may set in. On the other hand, if you are knowledgeable of the forest and the paths to take, it is easier and more joyful to navigate through the forest and thus find your way to the open space.

In this analogy, the paths represent the knowledge you have of yourself. When you know yourself well, you know better which path or paths to take and also you can better relate to the surrounding environment (the forest), which represents The Creator and all that is. When you understand and know yourself better, you can then better navigate through your life and thus have more joy and be at peace with The Creator and all that is. When you are in this space of joy and peace, your life flows easier. As your life flows easier, you are more aware of the steps and actions to take to accomplish your purpose in life, for you understand yourself better. It is not only the actions you take, but the state of being you choose to be in, that is, the state of mind and perspective you choose to live from, that helps to create the path for you to live your life in purpose.

Let us extend this analogy to include a river running through the forest. The river also represents The Creator, the source of all life. The river brings gifts of nourishment by providing water to drink and an avenue to travel in a way that is easier than walking. When you are in tune with and know yourself, you know which path to take through the forest and you can choose to use the river for easier and more restful traveling. When you know yourself better, you can more easily recognize the river as the vehicle to travel by; thus, you can "flow downstream on the river of life."

Those who may not know themselves well enough to navigate easily through the forest may happen upon the river, and perhaps in their confusion may try to travel on the river going upstream. We can all relate to how life goes when we go against the current. It is exhausting and filled with struggle. Compare this to traveling with the current, where life is easier and flows with less effort.

Exercise
Sit and contemplate this concept for a while. You may want to imagine yourself walking through the forest, knowing you have a great sense of yourself and thus are able to easily journey through the forest. Then see yourself as coming upon the river (for you know where it is) and seeing a wonderful and function-

al canoe. You sit in this canoe and travel down the river. How nice it is to see the blue sky and feel the perfect temperature. How calm and peaceful. Imagine the scenery. What do you see? Identify how you feel as you see the environment. Then be in tune with yourself and aware of your relationship with what you see. Start to examine how you feel being in this place and how you would feel if this was taken away. Take a pen and paper and write down your observations of yourself traveling down the river. Then sit and contemplate what surfaced from your writing.

You should be able to identify your relations and interconnection to the elements that came to your awareness through this exercise and you will easily see the elements of your life that are important and not important to you.

As you unravel the pieces that are connected to your life, you will discover more of who you are. For your life and all that it encompasses (people, circumstances, environment, and community) is a reflection of what is inside you. You can take this exercise and repeat it as often as you desire to focus on a specific area of your life, and use this tool to better understand elements about the area you are examining.

Here are a few helpful tips for using this exercise:

- Get into a meditative state.

- Set the intent to be given clarity on the topic you choose to examine.

- Be open to receive information given to you.

- Allow yourself to receive information without putting judgment on yourself, good or bad.

- Write down the information on a piece of paper.

At the end of the exercise, visualize yourself successfully getting out of the canoe and back on the path within the forest. You arrive at an open field where a crowd waits, cheering you on, for they are happy to see you. And you are happy to see them. You have succeeded in arriving from your path to your final destination.

Chapter 19
Recognizing the Interconnectivity of Life Creates Positive Outcomes

It is in the giving that you receive.

When you realize you carry the torch of all of humanity within you, and sense and feel the connection with all of life, you can celebrate the oneness and appreciate the connectivity that you are a part of. You can better understand and know in another person their pain and difficulties, for you are more aware and more in tune with them. You are better able to feel their joy for you have an appreciation for who they are. You are better able to withstand difficulties that sometimes arise between people because you see in them an aspect of yourself and therefore are better able to relate to them and their views.

When you have more compassion and reverence for Mother Earth, you can better relate to her and her difficulties. You can better enable your children to demonstrate the necessary consideration and reverence toward all of life when you demonstrate and model a life of love, compassion, awareness and connectivity to life.

You can better live in harmony with nature, other people and The Creator when you remember the connectivity of life, and also when you are connected within and know who you are. In addition, you live more in harmony when you live your life on purpose and are in a state of kindness, compassion, reverence, respect, love, support and creativity, which are different aspects of The One. Courage and fortitude is required, along with sincere interest and intent, to live a life coming from a place of connectivity that embraces the concept of unity.

Imagine what Utopia is like: the land of joy, peace, and harmony among all people. This is a place of utmost connectivity, in which you live in a state of self-love, and one that allows you to be comfortable to express fully who you are. As a result, you live your life with purpose, fulfilling the function or functions you are here to do. As a result, you see outside of yourself, your inner state of bliss, that is, there is an outpicturing of your inner being.

This state of bliss emanates to all around you, for all others are in the same state of being. We all recognize the divine nature in all and therefore demonstrate respect, love and understanding toward all life. When you treat yourself with kindness and respect, you are able to then give this, be this, and demonstrate this to others. A delightful way to be! Imagine your life in this way, and feel how this feels for you now. Extend this concept to being respectful and supportive of Mother Earth, and to her plants and animals. Sit with this for a while and use your imagination. Absorb the feelings within and contemplate, all the while, telling yourself that you choose to live in this way and are willing to start now.

Chapter 20
Trust and Surrender

You are the wonder of the universe, the central pivot of all.

You can consecrate yourself to The Creator and to the laws of the universe and in doing so you can become all the more enlightened with the presence of your being. What does this really mean? You live with great ease when you are in alignment with The Creator, for when you live purposefully from this place you are better able to flow with the river of life. When you do this, the circumstances and situations in your life fall into place. Using this analogy further, imagine that you are in a boat. This boat represents you and your life. The river is the ever-flowing Creator. When you relax, you float with the stream and when you are anxious, you feel you must control and paddle yourself on the river. Naturally when you paddle over a long period of time, you become tired and are no longer in the place of peace and relaxation for you need to rest. When you rest (surrender) then you are again more able to easily flow down on the river of life.

Imagine that you desire to change course, or direction, in your life. You can put out intentions and goals, take necessary steps to accomplish them, and find yourself steering toward the end result of what you set out to do. Entering the unknown and abandoning the known can cause anxiety but this can be avoided by knowing you are empowered, supported and guided by The One. Think of this. Realize the difference between this and being anxious. When you're anxious, you put out fearful thoughts and this creates waves in the river. For when we put fearful thoughts out we are saying the river is not holding us and we need to take control of the oars. When we do, we are exerting our own energy rather than being relaxed and surrendering to what is.

Recognize the difference between coming from a place of surrender and trust versus coming from fear and anxiousness. For if you know resources are always available for you to tap into, for if you know without a doubt that everything you need to accomplish is available, for if you have complete trust in the process of life, then you can relax and surrender to a better place. This causes the river to run more smoothly and the resources coming from the tributaries can better flow into the river. When you allow The Creator to have control you can more easily be your true authentic self. It is from this place of like vibration, of tandem living, that propagates, enables, and catalyzes the furthering of your life in the way it is meant to.

This brings us to the notion of free will. Free will means you *choose* how you want to live. Do you want to live from a place of trust and surrender or a place of control and fear?

Exercise
Think of a time in your life when you had great stress. What led to that stress? What arena (friendship, job, home, finances, relationship) of your life was this stress? As you contemplate the circumstances surrounding this stress, think of how you handled it. Did you take action toward reducing stress? Did you resolve the situation? What actions or situations occurred as a result of the steps you took? Did the stress go away, and if so, how quickly?

Spend a good amount of time thinking about this and try to assess if you came from a place of fear and control or a place of relaxing and surrendering. As you do this, realize there is no right or wrong way to your approach. You simply did the best you could. You always do.

Know and recognize that it was *your* choices that led to your actions (or non-actions). You can also see in this exercise the value of evaluating the different angles of the situation to fully appreciate all the resources that flowed into the river via tributaries. What elements helped you? Hindered you? What steps would you take today that would be different than before, if any? In what way did this situation serve you? What gift did you receive from this situation?

There are many avenues of resolving stress. But in the end, no matter what situation you are faced with, the bottom line is you *always* have a choice on how to react to it. Deeply know you have free will, and choose to use this free will to think and know that you are deeply cared for, provided for and always supported. Realize you can hold onto the towrope and receive assistance from The One as you so choose, or to do it alone. But it provides a much smoother and pleasant ride when you allow help from The One by relaxing, trusting and surrendering.

Close your eyes now and simply contemplate these notions, re-visiting the stressful situation you just assessed. Give yourself a lot of time to do this. As you do, be aware of emotions and feelings that may come up. Be gentle with yourself and don't judge. Observe your thoughts and feelings and be kind to yourself for having done the best you could do with the situation you were in.

If you so desire (now or at a later time) repeat the above exercise and assess a different stressful situation in a different part of your life. See if you handled it from a perspective of trust and relaxation or fear and control. Did you approach this stressful situation differently than the first situation? If so, was it because the circumstances were different or that you chose to approach it from a more spiritual per-spective. Or do you always approach situations like this in a similar manner? As you progress on your spiritual and personal journey it is quite likely that you will approach stressful situations from a place of trust and surrender.

Ask yourself what patterns you have regarding your approach to stressful situations. What can you do to minimize stress to be-gin with? Come into a place of deep knowing that you are doing the best you can, and as you continue to get to know yourself even more, you'll be able to recognize what action steps you can use to minimize the stress. Living in a place of surrender and trust will help minimize your stress, for you are more in a position to flow with the river of life and this helps create more ease by which you live.

Remember, the choice is always yours.

Chapter 21

The Necessity of the Expansion of Life

Variety of life is necessary to bring about the total purpose of The Creator, which is to express Itself.

Why is The Creator here to express? And what is Its self-expression? What purpose does it serve to be expressing and ever expanding? The answer is to get to know Itself.

You can express more in your daily life when you have a goal or purpose. It provides more of a foundation to stand upon so that you can then move forward with your existence. Without forward movement there is stagnation and in the stagnation there is no growth or expansion. You can appreciate this idea by considering what you would see if a child were to stay at a certain age without maturing. You can imagine the required energy it would take to stay put at a certain level, without expansion. The energy becomes denser within it and becomes stagnant. It is simply the law and nature of energy to become this way. The energy is there, but it becomes of such nature as to not move (in a way you and I know what movement is) and thus causes a stench. This is simply the best way to describe this situation. When energy has the opportunity to move and grow, when it can expand and free itself from stagnation, there is a more healthy aliveness and current that allows for more openness and freedom, more joy and interactivity with its environment.

When the child moves forward with his or her natural course of life's development the child will be able to flourish into his or her full capacity and expand and express his or her life in the unique way that is intended. There is an innate need to do this. In realizing that life is required to express itself, we can better appreciate the path of our own life and that of others, as well as of communities, cities, states, nations, and of the whole world. There are always interactions between the microcosm (an individual person) and the macrocosm (conglomerates and cities). Life flourishes within itself as it experiences the necessary interactions and interconnections with its surroundings (people, places, circumstances, the physical and nonphysical). No one flourishes and expands only by themselves; there is expansion and flourishing within the context of that person's environment and circumstances. The intertwining of all life with itself is what propels and helps move the whole of humanity forward on this planet. When you come to understand your place as part of the whole you can better appreciate yourself and what necessary gifts and talents you bring to the table. You can also better appreciate that every other person on the planet, including all other life forms interplay and interconnect with each other.

You can appreciate what goes on with The One when you realize the need and the requirement of forever expansion. This is the continuation of life, the flourishing and continual forward movement into the ever expansiveness of The One.

Golden Thread of Interconnection is Deep

The expansiveness of the universe is such that there continues to be the totality of all within itself yet there is ever expansion on the grand scale of The Creator. Try to comprehend this by visualizing The Creator as represented by the stars in the heavens above. Imagine The Creator is within all things and of all things, whether it is above in the stars, or the tiniest molecular structure. The interconnectivity within all will continue to expand upon itself more and more. When it expands upon itself, it then comes within itself, all the while moving forward and also moving inward. Life is within itself, ever expressing in the way it needs to express as a whole organism.

When you realize your nature to move forward and be ever expanding, you can better understand the nature of The Creator, for the two are indeed the same, all one. We all come from the same source of creation so we all experience the same experiences, albeit sometimes unconsciously, on the deepest levels of the soul. This is where the ever-residing planes of interconnectivity are truly felt. Deep within is the golden thread of interconnectivity. While you experience what you perceive as your individual self on the surface, on the deep level (the undercurrent) is the connection to all, connection of all—the interconnectivity, unity and "all-binding togetherness" nature of The One. *Deeply we are one!*

Meditation on Deep Interconnection
Meditate on this concept now, until you come to fully understand its meaning. Just relax into it. Set an intention to fully comprehend this idea. With sincere desire to do so, you will understand. As a result, you will have more stability and balance within your very essence. You may want to recall the analogy of the ocean and its droplets of water to better understand. The ocean is the ever-present connector (The Creator), and the drop of water from the ocean is the individualized expression (the individual person) that comes out to express. All the while, the ocean and the drop are the same, for they both come from, and are, The Creator.

Chapter 22
Emanating The Creator's Qualities and the Light Within You

Deeply know you are always held in the loving embrace of The One.

As the moon is a reflection of the sun's rays, we also reflect The Creator's light. For The Creator radiates from within each person. When we establish our connection to this source of light known as love, peace, joy, harmony, beauty, creativity, respect, kindness, and reverence we can better emanate and emulate the qualities of The Creator with our own being. We are that which emanates for The Creator, for we are the hands, hearts and healers of the giver of life to all.

Contemplate this concept. You can choose to emulate the qualities you most often attribute to The One through your own being. You then demonstrate these qualities to yourself and to others. What better way to live than in love, peace, joy, harmony, beauty, creativity, respect, kindness, and reverence within yourself and to have these radiate from you to others, and to radiate to all of life on our dear Mother Earth.

Sunbeam Meditation
Imagine living your life with self-love and kindness. How would you treat yourself? What would be typical of your self-talk? Would you be of peace and joy, and in true alignment with yourself and with The One? When you live your life with self-love and kindness, you achieve a more graceful state of being causing your life to flow with purpose and ease. When you are

in reverence for your own self, you are in reverence of The One and all of life on the planet and beyond.

Try this now. Come to a place of quiet and meditate on what it would feel like to love and respect yourself and to live in harmony and peace within yourself. Feel the joy that emanates from you as you feel the joy and peace within. Come to a place deep within that shines ever so brightly. Imagine a warm, bright light emanating from your heart to all those around you, as if you were the sun. Visualize the sunbeams radiating from your heart's center, growing longer and brighter with each breath. Be aware of how you feel as this sunbeam comes from you and reaches others in the form of love and peace. Feel these feelings. Be of quiet heart, deeply knowing that this is the will of The One for you to have this experience of love, peace, joy and harmony within and to share it with others.

Now imagine that as you emanate this love energy, it is radiating from your heart's center to others and that others are also radiating the same feelings. Now picture in your mind a whole room full of people being in this state. This is heaven on earth. Our lives are intended to live in love, peace, joy and harmony with all that is. Know that you can tap into your sunbeam at any time, knowing that if you so choose you can use this approach for living your day-to-day existence.

You can appreciate being in the space of The One as being a candle's flame. Imagine the flames of a million candles that are held together to create an image of the sun. When we divide this sun into a million holograms, we can imagine each individual flame as being its own light; the light of The Creator simply emanating from the perspective of an individual form.

How will you go about your day now with regards to sharing your gifts and talents, and living in love, peace, joy and harmony?

If your flame is burning low, what can you do to brighten it? Try the above meditation daily and use the following affirmation to help elevate the brightness of your flame: "Dear Creator of All, let me be of the deepest true knowing that I am indeed of You, that which is You, love, peace, joy and harmony. For I am one with You and You are one with me. Together we shine brightly. I deeply know this to be. And so it is."

Be willing to accept this as truth, even if it doesn't feel like it's true. Be willing to dissolve the old beliefs and old patterns that don't serve you. Be willing to become one with the flame of love and in doing so, the old beliefs and old patterns transmute to a neutral energy. Know your old beliefs are transformed and are no longer holding you back from the life you deserve. Celebrate that all is well and that you are transforming.

Contemplate this for a while and then revisit the state you were in before these exercises. Compare how you feel with the belief of being able to emanate these qualities of The Creator to how you felt prior to doing this. Be of kind heart to yourself for doing the best you can in your life, now and in the past. Be the biggest gift to yourself and have grace upon yourself; give yourself permission to cry if you need to, for the dismantling of old unneeded beliefs can bring to the surface of your awareness the emotions associated with them. These emotions need to be released, energetically, physically, mentally and in some cases spiritually.

Recognize you are *totally safe* and also *totally supported* by The Creator. If you can, be in tune with your emotions now. Gently lay aside your expectations and judgments of what you're experiencing and simply experience your emotions. You can also come to a place of quiet solitude and be with the emotions while journaling. This can help release that which does not serve you.

All is Truly Well for You

Be assured that all is well for you and you are in the place you need to be. All is in divine perfection in your life. There are gifts to receive from each experience; your willingness to accept this will help you see the gifts and thus help you further along your path of development and growth. Remember you are always in the loving arms of The Creator; The Creator is always guiding you; *you* are guiding you!

You can relax and be of great comfort in knowing that all your needs are met; all the elements and areas of your life are in place just as they need to be.

Be of good cheer, my dear soul, and recognize yourself as the divine, for you are indeed. Elevate your self-love and be kind to yourself; again giving yourself grace and love. Remember, you hold the same qualities as The One, which are love, peace, joy, harmony, beauty, creativity, respect, kindness, and reverence. Feel your heartbeat, your light that shines so brightly, your kindness and gentleness that really is ever present within you, for you are the hands, the heart and the eyes of The One. The One does work through you. The One is through you. The One is you. You are The One. Feel your flame, your light, radiating from yourself always. And so it is.

Chapter 23
Feed Your Life with Thoughts of Plenty

By examining what you see in your life, you can begin to realize you are the cause of your circumstances. You create your own reality.

Consider for a moment the result of your vitality and energy. What eating habits do you have that cause you to feel healthy and energetic, or to feel tired and lethargic? What activities do you partake in? How do you feel as a result of these activities? The outpicturing of your life is a result of your inner thoughts in the same way as your eating habits. What you put into yourself through eating creates the type of vitality, health and energy you experience. What you take in through your thoughts gets outpictured and manifested in the form of what you see as your life's circumstances, activities and situations.

So what would you like in your life? Feed your life with thoughts of plenty: "I am healthy!" "I always have more than enough money," "I have a wonderful job, spouse, partner, children, family," and "I live in great abundance." So on the contrary, if you feed your life with thoughts of lack "I *can't* get what I want," "I *don't* have a husband," "I *need* a better job," your life circumstances will mirror your thoughts. In other words, the result of your thoughts is what appears as your life.

Take Precious Care of Yourself
So how can you be a better steward of your own life? By thinking better thoughts, certainly, but also by making available to yourself ideas and what you desire to see in your life. You can better appreciate your thoughts by remembering to establish your circumstances by visualizing, by pretending and by using your imagination. To do this,

set an intention to establish a daily routine for yourself and make it a priority. Sit in contemplation as you decide what you'd like your life's circumstances to be. Then play! Go within and use your imagination to create your reality. Once you do this, you set thinking into motion for your life.

Chapter 24
How Thoughts Manifest onto the Physical Realm

Within The One is the knowledge of all.

We can appreciate the knowing of all life when we can appreciate ourselves better and in the same realm, begin to appreciate the goodness that comes forth into each person and the outpouring of this in the form of their unique gifts and talents. These unique gifts and talents are brought forth from the goodness within, which is really The One expressing itself through the individual person.

The Wheel Invention

Consider for a moment inventing the wheel. When the expression of this idea came forth, it was the divine intelligence, The One, which came through many people. This idea came forth first in thought, as all ideas do, and then with contemplation and fortitude, the mind's thoughts converted it to action, which was working with a piece of rock that eventually became the shape the person saw in their mind. When the rock was carved into a round shape, it was apparent that the "cycle of life" had become manifested. So we see, in this simple analogy, the outpouring of the idea that came to mind and passed through the physical body that then converted the piece of rock to the shape of a wheel.

Be aware that you can complete what you desire when you apply your creativity in a mindful way. For example, if you have the idea of the rock being a certain shape (circular) to accomplish what you desire (easier transport) and when you mindfully and thoughtfully consider how this may be accomplished, then you can more easily complete the task in the desired way. If, on the other hand, you were to not apply any thought, if you were to simply haphazardly cut away without applying a creative aspect to it, the rock could very well not turn into the desired shape. Instead, it would be of a shape (or lack of) that would not resemble what you had in mind. Consider this phrase "had in mind." This is exactly the literal and figurative speech to describe the process by which the thought comes into manifestation. "Had in mind" is the thought in your mind that allows the idea to manifest onto physical reality (form). There are mechanisms that allow what is in your mind to neurologically come forth from your mind (brain) to your hands, so you can convert or translate from the neurological brain impulse (thought) onto a physical vehicle, in this case your hands. Consider what this means. First there is an inspiration to create something. Then there is the idea in your mind which you then contemplate upon and consider how best to approach bringing it into manifestation. As this occurs, the brain stimulus is converted through your physical vehicle and the idea gets outpictured, that is, created onto the physical realm. This illustration demonstrates how unmanifested thought comes into the manifest/physical realm.

Manifesting Your Desires

When you apply the concept of manifesting your desires to the next level, you know that as your ideas (thoughts) are put forth onto the ether or stratosphere of The One Mind/The Creator, they are being converted to a wave length of energy that begins to take form onto the physical plane and becomes manifested. This occurs in the manner in which we have put out your ideas or images. In order to be more certain that you bring forth your desired outcome, you must carefully assess your thoughts to be sure they're appropriate to creating your desires and intentions.

What is being demonstrated here is the outpicturing of such desires as a soul mate, successful business, or a summer home. You put the image out there to The Creator in a manner that is most applicable to your life. These thoughts go onto the ether and as they do, if the vibration of this is revisited a number of times, and if there is sincere desire to manifest the thoughts, the vibrations will conglomerate with each other to form the physical manifestation of your desires. This outpicturing encompasses the highest form of the idea, that which is most useful in accomplishing your desired outcome. Keep in mind that the resulting manifestation is for the best of everyone concerned so there are angles and aspects of the outcome that may not completely, at least to you, represent the desired outcome in *exactly* the way you envisioned it, but to The Creator, it matches exactly. The manifestation comes forth in the highest level of what is good for *all* and completely fulfills the purpose of that desired outcome.

Keep in mind that if you are having repeated thoughts of something that you *don't* want, the mechanism of creating them is the same as just described. The manifestation is simply occurring from an *unconscious* place. Therefore, to create what you really desire (rather than what you don't desire), it is vital to be *consciously aware* of your thoughts, your self-talk, your attitude, your perspective and your feelings. And, when you add sincere desire and intent behind your thoughts, the creative process is all the more effective.

Our Highest and Best Good

How many times have you heard someone say they wanted to create something from an idea they had, only to find out later that the idea did not manifest in the form they expected. Hopefully they recognized that it manifested perfectly just the way it did and always for our highest and best good. We can illustrate this through example. Suppose you desire a soul mate, so you think positive thoughts about it, believing that this is possible to have in your life. Then you let go of these thoughts and put them to rest, recognizing that letting go and surrendering this allows for easier manifestation. In awhile, you meet someone who seems to be a good fit and through getting to know this person, you realize he or she is not the soul mate you had intended. Does this mean the manifestation of your desire did not occur? No, what it means is you have gotten closer to understanding yourself better. How? As you get to know this person, you are also getting to know yourself; you are seeing a reflection of yourself in the

93

other person. Remember, that which is inside you is what you see outside yourself. You saw a mirror (an outpicturing) of yourself in this person. This is the gift of meeting this person, who was the result of the manifestation of your desire. As a result, you are closer to meeting your soul mate because now you are better able to put out new and appropriate vibrational frequencies to the universe, the ether, (in the form of thoughts) so that the possibility for the manifestation of what you truly desire will come forth in a more clearly defined physical reality. Through this process, you will be better able to manifest a relationship with your soul mate.

You can see through the process of putting forth your ideas, they can come back to you as you desired. The timing may not always be what you wanted, and the manifestation may not always be exactly what you expected, but the ideas and thoughts will manifest for the highest and best possible way to achieve the best and greatest results for your life.

You can begin to imagine the creative forces that come forth from you, as well as creative ideas and inspirations that come to you, and appreciate the co-creative processes that are always at play in the realms of what you know to be your life!

Be of great mind and heart!

Chapter 25
Moments of Despair Can Be Moments of Enlightenment

Open your heart in a manner that brings you peace which brings you in union with The One and when you are in union with The One, you bring yourself peace.

What can you do when your heart is heavy, and your thoughts have brought you down? What can you do to remind yourself to come back to The One, to come back to the place of center and connection with The One that will bring you the peace and joy you desire and deserve? You can begin by invoking your anchor and also remembering who you are. Or you could go to your sanctuary while meditating or looking intently at the picture that reminds you of your place of center or singing your special song. You could simply be with yourself and with a quiet mind, gently talking with yourself as if you are your best friend, sincerely bringing kindness and love to yourself all the while allowing yourself to receive. Receive the kind words and receive the sensation of love. Allow yourself to receive the invitation to uplift yourself, knowing it is your rightful place to be of peace and joy. Allow yourself to believe it is your divine right to be peaceful and joyful.

Opportunities to Delve Deeper

Many times we think being in a place of upset is not the place to explore, but in fact it gives us the opportunity to delve deeper into our being and is a portal into part of our personality. Even moments of despair can be considered moments of enlightenment. They help you gain insight into what is beneath the surface. When it is properly held in the light of The One, and you understand that this part is also who you are, you can more easily embrace this aspect of yourself. It is important to remember that you are only in this place of discord for a short while and that you have techniques, as mentioned above, to move toward peace and joy. It is also important to remember that all aspects of who you are come from within, which is to say that it comes from The Creator. When you surrender yourself to the knowing that all is well, and that *all* aspects of you (positive and negative) are part of you, then you can accept, embrace and own yourself more fully. You are then kinder and gentler and pour forth more easily the grace upon yourself.

To illustrate this, let us use an example of a young woman who is outgoing and has many friends. She has many occasions to experience her gifts and talents, two of which are singing and dancing, which she loves to do. Professional people are interested in her talent. But deep within, she has insecurities of being successful, although this is unknown to others. She recognizes her insecurity for success in the singing and dancing arena and has chosen to meditate for inner guidance on this. She realizes she's not successful because she doesn't follow through with completing tasks and projects and she has berated and scolded herself for this. This contributes to her not moving forward with her singing and dancing career.

The issue as to why she doesn't complete a task or project also needs to be explored. She realizes a self-sabotage developed at a very young age, through her upbringing, that led her to believe that she cannot accomplish her desires because of unfounded inadequacies so she believes she doesn't deserve to have the things she wants.

Through recognizing this, she can realize she deserves what she desires. She needs to embrace this part of herself, the part that believes she doesn't deserve to have what she wants and also the part that longs for success. Through some work and awareness on her part, she can begin to embrace this negative aspect and cradle it with love.

Once she has the courage to move forward with singing and dancing auditions, she will be able to accomplish her goal of receiving what she desires and at the same time, recognize and embrace the old patterns.

You can see from this simple illustration the necessity of being aware of past patterns and negative or false beliefs and to break through them as needed so you can fully live your life.

It is important to recognize and be aware of the old patterns as they come up. This is the key and is of utmost importance, for when you are aware of them then you can more easily shed your light of consciousness on them and get back to center, thus back into joy and peace. Remember to be kind and gentle with yourself.

Embrace all parts of yourself, even the old patterns or what you may consider negative personality traits (also known as shadow sides). Acknowledge and praise yourself for being aware that your old patterns are important, for it is the awareness that allows you the freedom to choose to go back to the place of center and connection to The One and away from the place of discord.

It is this awareness that brings forth the ability to live in a more awakened and loving presence in your existence.

Chapter 26
Love Essence

Love is the highest form of The One, the highest and sweetest vibration there is. We are created from this love and therefore we are love; this is our true essence.

When you create within yourself the sincere desire to live in harmony with others, with the earth and with yourself, you are better able to flow with life with ease and grace. You are better able to demonstrate that which you are really here for, truly harmonizing yourself with your true essence: love. For love is the ultimate vibration, the highest form and the only form, of The One. Imagine living your life from a place of love. From here you see and *know* the true essence of who you are, you respect and love yourself, are kind to yourself, and have healthy boundaries with others. As a result, you are more able to bring forth kindness, understanding, respect and love to others. This is because you have the building blocks within yourself (loving and respecting yourself) to share it with others. Imagine how you would feel living in this manner.

Exercise
Close your eyes and imagine what you feel like when you are kind, loving and respectful to yourself. Remember a time when someone treated you like this. How did you feel? You felt cared for and loved. You felt good. You probably had a sense of warmth and wholeness about yourself. You probably returned this love and respect to the other person. When we can be in this place of love for an extended period of time, the love has a way of building upon itself. Now, as you continue to remember this state of love, also remember how this feeling or space was maintained. You may not remember, for this is not something that can be forced or worked for. It is not something you need

to make happen. It is, however, a feeling that naturally occurs if you are open, aware and in tune with yourself. Recognize that when you live from an orientation of respect, love, kindness and reverence for life, you are more able to be in the space of The One, for these are the qualities of The Creator. These are attributes that are in alignment with the highest vibrations in all of existence. You don't need to use force to get these vibrations. These are natural vibrations that are easy to maintain, once you have the proper foundation.

Recognize there is a deep conditioning through your culture and upbringing that can create a blockage or resistance to dismantling the very thing that needs to be dismantled, and that is the ego. The ego, as you may recall, is here as part of the oneness, but due to its lower vibratory nature it seems to be in separation and will not as easily assimilate the higher vibration of love. It needs to be coaxed into and to be brought into a neutral state, so we can invoke the true and higher vibration we know as love. The true essence of love comes from the heart, whereas the ego-based love comes from the mind. Being aware of yourself will help you distinguish between these two and will assist you in coming from the place of the heart.

Meditation with the Qualities of The Creator
To step into this arena of love, respect and reverence, begin by going into a quiet meditation and set the following intent for yourself "I intend and deeply know my true nature is that of The One, and since I am part of The One, and The One has the qualities of love, beauty, harmony, peace, joy, respect, kindness, creativity and reverence, I too have these attributes. My intention is to bring these forth now."

Sit with and feel these attributes inside you. Pick one or two to begin with. Make believe if you need to. Play with and enjoy the feelings and know them to be true. Recognize you're making a conscious choice to feel and bring these positive qualities to you. This is the most important aspect of this exercise. Be in the knowing that you can, at any time, be in this place.

Feeling Love in Your Daily Life

It may not be so easy to stay in this place. Certainly it's easy to stay here when you are focusing on being here, but what about when you go about your daily life? Where you are experiencing life and everyone and everything has their own energy creating distractions and challenging your will.

It is easier to maintain this space of love and reverence for life when you hold in your heart what it feels like. Also, there are several techniques you can do to more easily invoke these feelings, such as the following:

- You can be loving and kind to yourself. To invoke this, you simply act as if you are talking to your own best friend with compassion and understanding whenever you are talking with yourself. Look in the mirror and tell yourself loving words, such as "I look wonderful today!" or "Great job I did yesterday" or "I am feeling strong and healthy." Talk with yourself with sincerity and love, as if you are in love with yourself (as it ought to be!).Try this several times a day and feel yourself believing it.

- You can use the affirmation "I and The Creator are one. We are of like mind and heart. Therefore I am love, peace, joy, harmony, kindness and beauty."

- As you go about your day, you can invoke the space of love by being totally present with yourself, with the person you are with, or the circumstances you find yourself in. For example, you find yourself in a hurry at the grocery store and the checkout line is taking a long time. You start to feel yourself becoming impatient or frustrated. Bring yourself into the present moment and accept the fact that this is what it is. Simply stop resisting and take a deep breath. Allow the feeling of love to come forth from your heart and sense the peace that comes forth. With practice, you will find that small aggravations will become less or nonexistent while peace fills your heart.

- Visualize a warmth emanating from your heart, and feel how it warms your insides with the glow of love and peace.

- See the beauty of a flower or a butterfly or the glorious colors of a sunrise or sunset; the harmony of the birds as they fly in unison; the majestic mountains, or the gentle waves of the ocean. Be truly at one with whichever of the five senses you are using. Be acutely aware of your sensations and feel present in the moment. When you're in the present moment, it's easier to be in the space of love, harmony, peace, joy and reverence for life. When you can be completely with the experience of your five senses and truly relish in it, you will experience the exquisite state of love.

Try a number of these techniques throughout the day today and see for yourself how easy it is to invoke the feeling and space of love into your life. To more effectively invoke the feeling of love, it helps tremendously to be in a state of awareness, that is, to live consciously. Live in a state of awareness of your environment, your body, your feelings, and your effect on others. As you live from a place of awareness, you will appreciate the essence of who you are here on earth, as part of the vastness of all of life.

Invoking the feeling of love can be done anywhere. Remember you have the power to choose your thoughts and to choose to do this at any time. Just stop your negative thoughts and make a conscious choice to shift into the feeling and space of love.

When you are more in this space of love, peace, harmony, joy and reverence for life, you are then better able to extend this to those around you, as well as to the environment, plants and animals. How will you treat others when you are in the space of love? How will you respond to others? Imagine now, in meditation, what it's like to have happy, healthy, loving, respectful, kind and peaceful interactions with others. Sit with this and relish the feelings you have of this type of interaction, this type of living. Visualize how easy it is to go about your day in this state of love. And imagine the other person acting and being in the same space as you. How pleasant! Sit with this for a while and enjoy.

Chapter 27

Creating an Atmosphere of Courtesy and Respect with Others

You are always in a better place when you can appreciate yourself more and bestow loving kindness upon yourself. This then easily radiates to others.

What do you suppose would be created in an interaction between two people when both are coming from the space of love and kindness and when both are being respectful and courteous toward one another? What would it be like when both are being aware of themselves and their own shortcomings; are aware of the rules and policies they abide by, recognize their own established routines and their own way of doing things and are aware of their gifts, talents and their personality traits? When you have a true knowing of yourself and a sense of ownership of your own being, a deep understanding can occur when you interact with others. It is as if the reason for getting together is to share in an activity that brings both people a sense of joy and camaraderie. Of course, this can happen socially, in business, or family matters. Keep in mind that the talents of the two people interacting with each other play a vital role in the outcome of their interaction. For when there is a basis of love and respect, each person is better able to provide an opening for the other person to be their authentic self. When you feel comfortable with yourself, you can allow and create the space for the other person to also feel comfortable to authentically express themselves. This is the start of an interaction driven by authenticity

Kate Heartsong

Extend this concept to the idea of allowing the other to express his or her ideas without your judgment, allowing the other to truly be who they are, even if it means it is counter to what you believe. For what harm is it to be in the presence of another who has a different opinion than you? The result of having two different opinions may be inconsequential.

In the case where there are two differing opinions where only one of the opinions can be used, it is important to focus on the end result, that is, on the common purpose, of the two people getting together. The end result has the priority over who feels right in their opinion. For if you were to focus on who feels right, there is a possibility of disrespect or nonsupport. Ideally, when *both* people come together intending to find the best end result, a space of respect and love is easier to create. It is the focus you choose to put your attention to, that is your perspective, which helps to guide you and helps you propagate a space of mutual respect and love. For when you can come from this vantage point, doing what's best for the optimal outcome, you can better allow the people involved to be who they are meant to be.

You can also help the situation at hand by allowing yourself to express your gifts, and by allowing others to do the same. As you express what is inside you, it is easier for others to express what is inside them, allowing their authentic selves to emerge into the glory of who they are. When you are in your own truth, others can more easily feel comfortable in their own truth. You can extend this to recognize the unity and interconnectivity between yourself and others. For while you have your own unique gifts, talents, and personality, you also strive to be aware that you are from the same source, from The One, and in this, recognize the common thread that holds us together— love. This assists you in a better understanding of all people.

It is important to remember that all people desire respect, understanding and support from a place of nonjudgmental values. It is a starting point in any communication or interaction which creates a

106

better space for the interaction to take place. You more easily allow each person to be who they authentically are, as well as allowing this for yourself.

Exercise
Contemplate this and absorb its meaning for a while. Then do the following exercise: Imagine being with a person where you need to conduct a business meeting. Imagine the purpose of this meeting is to solve a problem. Both of you are knowledgeable about the problem and both of you have solutions to it, but only one solution can be offered. Imagine yourself listening to the other person. How does it feel to you if this person's idea is, in your opinion, not feasible? Then offer your solution. See how the other person responds to your solution. Set up the scenario that you are both allowing for the space of your meeting to be such that there is mutual respect for each other, and that the optimal end result is what is most important to both of you. How does your interaction proceed? How do you feel? How do you think the other person feels?

Do your best to be an observer of this interaction, pretending it is ideal, that the best solution is chosen, not because one person's idea is better than another, but that the solution happens to be the best fit to create the optimal end result.

Observe as well how you react and respond if your solution is not chosen. This can give you valuable insight into who you are pertaining to situations involving conflict resolutions. How willing are you to listen to the other person's solution? How attached are you to your idea? Is there a better way for you to deal with this situation? Do you feel comfortable with yourself? How much do you help create an atmosphere that allows the other person to feel at ease and thus be more able to express his or her ideas?

There are many insights you can receive from this. When you do this exercise, it is useful for you to be with it for as long as you can, to give you a feel for where you are in this sort of scenario. If you desire, start keeping a journal of notes from real interactions you have

Kate Heartsong

with others, and log answers to the questions presented above. Be open to what you observe regarding yourself, and be gentle, kind and respectful to yourself in your observations.

If you find yourself critical of your behavior, assess why you're being critical. Do you feel the need to improve yourself or are you chastising yourself because you don't think you are capable of being respected? If you are being unkind to yourself, bring yourself back to center and connection with The One, and fully love and respect yourself.

Chapter 28
Trusting and Creating Positive Thoughts

Having the foundation of trust and faith will always carry you forth in such grand glory you will be uplifted and exalted to your very essence.

Recall that you can choose to have certain positive thoughts and you can steer clear of thoughts that don't positively serve you. Remember, you are at choice at all times. This helps you live more consciously. When you live more consciously, it's easier to step into a choice-oriented life, in which you choose to be, act, and think in certain positive ways rather than existing in a reactive mode.

Imagine being in a happy mood, where you know ahead of time the bounty of abundance that will be bestowed upon you that day. Imagine being aware of your feelings, listening to and following your inner guidance, and sharing your light with others with the joy and peace you have within you. When you do, you radiate the glow within you to others. You share your gifts and talents with others from a place of love and heartfelt compassion. Living this way helps spread peace. This is because of your effect on others and on yourself when you live from this place. It is a matter of energies and vibrations emanating from your being that naturally—it is law—overlaps onto another person's essence, aura, or being.

Like Attracts Like
Imagine that you are worried about getting a job. There is a person you run into who knows of a job opening where he works and you are excited to apply for it but share with him your belief that it's difficult to get a job. You decide to apply for the position and are relieved

to get an interview. You relax into believing there's an opportunity here. But you have had for a long time deep concerns of not receiving the job. Your inner belief is that it is difficult to obtain employment and the vibration of this belief has been put forth for some time onto the universe/ether and this impacts the employment process because like thoughts vibrationally match up with like circumstances. You end up not obtaining this position; therefore, you once again have demonstrated to yourself the belief that it is difficult to obtain a job.

On the other hand, when you have many positive thoughts and choose to believe it is easy to obtain a job, you send out vibrations to the universe/ether that attract like vibrations and this will create circumstances that match your beliefs. As a result, you find that obtaining a job is easier. When you choose to have a positive attitude, in spite of what you see in your surrounding environment, you are able to find a match of equal or similar vibration that brings you the circumstances of what you have inside yourself (in this case, the ease or difficulty of being hired). Once again, recognize that your thoughts become your experiences. It is the circumstances and events in your life that are reflections of what is inside you. So why not choose pleasant and positive thoughts and feelings? Having the choice of positive thoughts and feelings makes it easier to live the life you desire.

Trust Your Inner Guidance

It is the soul within that is guiding you toward the direction you desire. So in the case of trying to obtain a job, when you listen to your soul's inner guidance, when you relinquish control by trusting and by flowing with the river of life, and when you relax in the knowing that you can choose to have these types of thoughts, then you are in a much better position to obtain a job (or anything in life) that is for your highest good.

So what is required to be in a place of trust? What can you do to exercise your mind, your brain, and your heart into believing a more positive reality?

- Begin each day by connecting to yourself and having gratitude for who and what you are. Recall the gifts and talents you have to offer the world. Be with this feeling of appreciation for yourself, and find peace in yourself. Become at one with yourself by loving and appreciating yourself more. As you do, you build more trust within yourself. Building trust with yourself is crucial and will help you build trust in all processes of life.

- Begin a daily practice of meditation, for doing this enables you to be more in touch with yourself and with The One. In doing so you are able to accept the truth of who you are, which is a magnificent being upon this earth. As you build your self-confidence, you are, again, able to trust yourself and also have better energy vibrations that are, in turn, felt by others. This positive energy attracts others causing better interactions in your daily life because they pick up on your positive energy essence (like attracts like) and you will soon begin to experience more positive experiences. One of them can very well be obtaining the job you've been seeking.

- Create a special altar in your home that is specific to your heart's desires. This altar can consist of special mementos that bring a sense of peace and joy. It could include such items as a sentimental family photo, a unique rock from a place that brought you joy on vacation, a poem, or picture that ignites a certain pleasant memory; anything that brings you a feeling of love and warmth can be put on your altar. Once you have this altar, sit next to it and just be with the essence of it. As you are with these objects, choose to have positive thoughts, and choose to relax and trust all is well.

- You can carry with you a small cherished object that warms your heart and reminds you that all *is* well for you.

Touch this object during the day as often as you like. As you touch the object, you can *feel* in your heart and say any of the following words to help build trust:

-   I am a child of The Creator and this inherently means I am indeed taken care of on all levels. All my needs are easily met.

-   It is The One whom I am always with and therefore I trust that all is well in my life.

-   I fully know and believe that all I need is provided for me now and always. I deeply breathe this truth into my soul.

-   The Creator, You and I are one, and therefore abundance of joy, peace, and harmony are mine. I easily receive these blessings.

These are but a few examples of what you can say to yourself. You can make up your own; the important thing is to be diligent and include references that remind you to be trusting.

Remember you always have choice in your thoughts. Use sincere desire and intent to build more trust within yourself thereby overriding any old conditioned patterns or beliefs. Recognize that there are old beliefs that you may not be aware of, but when you apply your mind and you apply your co-creative power with sincere intent to do good for your life (in this case to build strong trust) then you are better able to eradicate and dissolve the old false beliefs that do not serve you.

Using the above suggestions is effective because you are in a better position to dismantle the old beliefs. This is due to your position in the evolution of human kind. You are energetically more able to eliminate old beliefs because they have been primed and softened to be more easily dissolved. The healing of old wounds and old false beliefs is much faster now than it used to be, for the ego's grip is no longer as strong.

When you have a deep knowing that all is provided for you, when you increase your trust that all is well, when you let go of the oars of your river boat and let your inner guidance lead the way, then you have greater joy and peace within. This then radiates out to others. You benefit and others benefit. So do animals, plants, and the whole of Mother Earth.

In the end, you find true joy and peace within yourself through trust and faith and being truly authentic. Completely embracing this concept brings you to a place of living your life the way it is meant to be lived: expressing the truth of who you are, which is The One expressing through you.

Chapter 29
Living Authentically

Authenticity is the key to flourishing and living in the capacity of your maximum potential. It encourages and propels you into the unfoldment of your life as it is meant to be unfolded.

We want you to discover the path to your richest life. We want you to be at peace with of all life. We want you to experience the blissful nature of the Divine, The Creator—in doing so you will then flow with the river of life, making it more conducive for your authentic self to flourish. We have spoken of the need to be living authentically, to know that when you live from the place of your true nature you are then better able to give of yourself to the infrastructure of life, to all the interconnectivity of the universe.

You can best help propagate living your authentic self by becoming aware of yourself and who you are as a person. Know your gifts, talents and personality; be aware of your body's sensations, your emotions, and the impact you have on others and on Mother Earth. Here are some useful tools that will help promote living from this place of authenticity and conscious living.

Awakening Your Authenticity

In a special journal, describe what you experience throughout each day, making general observations of your accomplishments and activities. Observe and evaluate any situations you had that were more significant or meaningful to you. In doing so, be aware of how you approached this, or how you presented yourself in this situation, then list in your journal what gifts or attributes were evident in your experience. Be aware of whatever reactions you may have had. Also become more aware of how you show up in your daily life and how you show up in different, unusual, or special circumstances. Be with this for a few minutes each day and it can help you be aware of any patterns or habits you may have. Keeping this journal helps you have more insight to yourself and will help promote self-awareness.

For example, if you are the type of person who is shy but would like to be a bit more outgoing and have more interactions with others, you might recognize this by writing down observations of yourself. Maybe you notice that you are quiet when a certain person comes into your office at work. As you write your observation that evening, you find that you are particularly shy with this person. As you assess this, you may ask yourself what is it about this person that causes you to become shyer. Perhaps you realize it is because that person reminds you of your father, who taught you to be quiet in the presence of male authority figures. Recognizing this is insightful and does present the gift of being able to live more consciously and in more awareness of why you act and react as you do.

When you recognize and embrace that you live in the now, and not in the past, you are able to live in a present place of confidence. You can then be less shy (if this is your desire). With the observation about yourself, you can shine the light of consciousness on the situation and choose to make a change in your interaction.

This example is a simple illustration of the benefits we receive by observing and assessing how we show up each day and how we interact with others.

Another tool that will help you be more authentic is to be truthful with yourself. Be honest with yourself. You can apply this by being aware of your moods and the way you feel. Be aware of how you feel with a particular person. Be truthful with yourself on how you feel toward that person. Do you enjoy being with this person? Interactions with others are always helpful in bringing you information about yourself and about who you are. It is insightful to see what is in the mirror. When you can assess your feelings and emotions in an honest way, you are able to live with truth and authenticity.

Exercise
Try this with the next person you encounter. Simply observe how you feel, being completely honest with what you feel, noting this in your journal. Recognize any patterns you may have with that person. By being in tune with your feelings, you can get a better sense for who you are. For example, if you feel doubtful or untrusting when you are with a certain person, you can then honestly ask yourself why you feel this way and have courage to realize that it is a reflection of your own self-doubt. By doing this, you gain insight into yourself, recognizing the reflection you see is the mirror, which brings to light what is inside you. Then you can choose, if you desire, to explore why you have doubt and take action to overcome this.

All that is required to change is contemplation, courage, honesty, and a willingness to change. When you are willing to do this work and to evaluate situations, you are well on your way to knowing yourself better and therefore are more able to be your authentic self. You are here for the purpose of fulfilling your destiny by being who you are, that is by bringing forth your authentic self. You have a specific function that is vital to all of life, for if you didn't you wouldn't be here to begin with.

As you accomplish your purpose by living in an authentic manner, you help build the infrastructure of all life. Each person within the whole of humanity has a vital purpose within the function of the planet. The purpose of Mother Earth is to express herself as the keeper and maintainer of life that she houses. And in her glory of fulfilling her function, the children, plants and animals reap the benefits. The benefit of Mother Earth is her bounty and abundance, and she freely gives this to all life.

Uncovering the Essence of Who You Are

When we speak of the authenticity in the infrastructure of humanity, we are speaking of the way life presents itself naturally and organically. But there are circumstances, cultural teachings and learned behaviors that muddy up the authenticity of your essence. It is therefore more difficult to shine your true essence when you experience the different conditioned patterns that you learned from your culture, as well as the individualized conditioning coming from within the family unit. When you are taught through reward and punishment as a means to properly behave and express yourself, you are molded into the very being that often disallows your authentic self-expression. You become accustomed to behaving in ways that please others, and often this can be to the degree that you compromise your authentic self, to a point that "hides" or covers up who you really are.

How can you express your authentic self even though you have conditioned experiences that have covered up your true self? You can begin dismantling your conditioned behavior by remembering that you come from The Creator. It is beneficial to see yourself in the light that you truly are, which is absolute divine nature, and recall that The Creator expresses Itself through you.

When you live and feel your connection with The One, you are able to experience, and be, the qualities of The One, which are peace, joy, love, harmony, beauty, creativity, respect, reverence and kindness. This also assists in dismantling conditioned behaviors that have covered your true, authentic self. Meditate to bring yourself to your connection with The One. When you are meditating deeply, you feel a sense of calm, peace and joy. You may also feel being at one with all, or at least you feel your essence expand, to the point where you don't know where your essence/energy ends and the environment's essence/energy begins.

When you know yourself better, appreciate yourself more, care and love yourself more, you can express yourself in a more authentic manner. Remember also to include the elements of self-confidence, self-honoring, self-respect and self-kindness. Living like this further enables you to express yourself authentically with yourself and with others, and assists you in expressing your life's purpose. If everyone lived their life's purpose, it would fit well together in the infrastructure of life. This interconnectivity is required to further the larger purpose, and that is the ever-changing, ever-expansion of The Creator.

Remember again that the function or purpose of all life is to express itself fully, and to bring forth the qualities of The One. Examples of these are the kindness and expression of the love of a mother to her child, the kindness a neighbor shows to a lost dog or a neighborhood project that helps the homeless. There are countless other activities and acts that help others in ways that enable them to become their authentic selves. It is all in the name of The One.

Chapter 30
The Ripple Effects of Living Authentically

The best way to live your essence is to be the essence of The Creator.

When you realize you live in a place of not being authentic, you can find peace within by bringing yourself into alignment with The One. Simply being in the light and awareness of your non-authenticity helps resolve it, and can bring you into your own essence. You can choose to have a sincere desire and intent to live authentically. Understand that you can align yourself with your essence, your authenticity, by meditating and connecting with The One. Meditation is frequently suggested because it is a simple and effective way to bring yourself to the place of connection. It helps to still and quiet the monkey mind or chatter. And in silence, you can then know The One, yourself.

Exercise
Contemplate why meditation is so effective. Sit with this notion and consider deeply the reason why being with The One enables you to live your life in more fullness. Also be aware of the calming effects it causes on your physical, mental and emotional aspects of your being. When you are in a place of complete stillness your thoughts are more clear, have more clarity, and it's easier to see from a higher-level perspective, your higher self or soul. You are better able to be a witness to your thoughts and actions and live a much more conscious life; that is, you are better able to live in a more positive and acute state of awareness. This leads to accessing your intuition (inner wisdom) better, which enables you to easily connect to the Divine Intelligence of The One, which in turn helps deepen your con-

nection to It. With this connection, you reap the benefits of easily traveling and flowing on the river of life.

The Domino Effect

You are better able to live from a place of authenticity when you live from a place of connectivity with The Creator. Furthermore, as you arise to this place of connectivity (authenticity), you'll see that you have a more positive influence on others. You are able to live in harmony and understanding with your fellow human beings. You are able to live from a vantage point of having a high level of reverence for all life and are able to live with more caring and compassion. You are more apt to live from a place of respect for all people, animals, plants and Mother Earth. Imagine if all of us were able to live in this place. It would be a better environment, one conducive to harmony, peace, and joy.

You can appreciate how living an authentic life facilitates your life to flow more smoothly and helps you contribute your gifts and talents to the whole. At the same time, your authenticity facilitates creating a more peaceful world. The interconnectivity between people is better understood as well, thus respect and harmony have a ripe environment to flourish. It is the very nature from which harmony, peace and respect reside, that then surface, bloom and comes forth. What can you do, then, in addition to meditation, that promotes your authenticity? Try the following suggestions:

- Know yourself to the fullest through understanding your gifts, talents and personality.

- Appreciate and love yourself.

- Listen to your inner voice (your intuition) and follow through with the guidance you receive.

- Follow your heart.

- Be in tune with your body and its wisdom.

- Be aware of your moods and emotions.

  When several or all of these elements are woven into the fabric of your being, it allows for a more authentic you.

Awareness

It may seem overwhelming to try to remember all of these suggestions, but they come easily just by being aware. It is important to have awareness of your body, your thoughts, your feelings, your effect on others and the environment, and to have awareness of your connection with The Creator. With practice, living from a place of awareness becomes natural.

Here are some tips to practice living from a place of awareness:

- Bring yourself to the present moment. If you catch yourself thinking of the past or worrying about the future, then gently recognize it and focus instead on where you are standing or sitting at the moment. Remind yourself of what you are presently doing and do your best to stay present with it.

- Focus on the *goal* of your present activity. Ask, "Why am I doing what I'm doing now?" It could be you are grocery shopping and although your purpose of grocery shopping is obvious, stopping and asking this question helps bring you into the awareness of what you're currently doing. This encourages your being present.

- Stop and observe your thoughts. By doing this, you become more aware of yourself and what you are thinking.

- Observe yourself. Be aware of your mood, feelings, emotions and physical body.

You can easily incorporate any or all of these many times a day to help you be more aware. Remember, being more aware will help you live more consciously. And this, in turn, helps you live in a more present, alert state, which facilitates your connection to The One. This helps facilitate living with more joy and peace and elevates your positive effect on others, which can positively affect the larger environment you're in. Imagine tens of thousands, millions of people being in this place of awareness! There is a better respect for all of life, for the unity of life, for the reverence of life.

What are the benefits of living your life from a place of connection with The Creator? It gives you a better vantage point to perceive life, your life and life as a whole. It allows you to better appreciate your effect on yourself and others. How? By appreciating yourself, you can then appreciate others. When you can better appreciate yourself, you can better acknowledge the beauty of the divine nature of all that is, for that which is within you can then better be brought forth and be seen outside of yourself. That which is *not* within you, cannot be put forth outside (outpictured) for it's just not there to be put forth.

Positive Influences of High Self-Esteem
Imagine living a life that does not allow for you to express your authentic self. This would be stifling. You would have a difficult time remembering who you truly are. You would go around living from a place of reaction rather than a place of joy and awareness. And what kind of life is it that is not conscious? How can you appreciate yourself and others when you are not in tune with your gifts and talents? Too many people live their life in difficulty because they are merely trying to survive and they don't appreciate themselves or what they have. They aren't aware they are divine so they don't treat themselves well. How can they treat others well if it's not within them to begin with? They can't.

This is why it's vital that you do appreciate and love yourself and that you begin to acknowledge your own grandness, and to lift up your self-esteem. Seeing yourself as divine will help increase your sense of self-worth. And this, of course, leads to feeling better about yourself, which in turn helps you to better appreciate yourself. You then can easier live in a more relaxed and joyous state and know the positive effects this has toward you, toward others and toward Mother Earth and all her inhabitants.

It is not always easy to apply these suggestions to everyday life because you are busy. This is why it is imperative you remind yourself frequently to apply these suggestions.

Practice these suggestions every day to bring yourself to a higher self-esteem:

- Look in the mirror and just appreciate the person you see. Allow yourself to receive this appreciation.

- Be mindful of your self-talk. Avoid self-criticism. Use positive self-talk.

- Buy a special book or something that allows you to spend time alone, nurturing yourself.

- Seek a counselor if you feel you need professional assistance with raising your self-esteem.

- Know that elevating your self-esteem takes time, and know that it is indeed possible. Remember to set the sincere desire and intent to do so.

Chapter 31
Fulfilling Your Life's Purpose

How sweet it is to sing your heart's song to the world, and to yourself!

When an individual complains of a headache, the headache is still there, for complaining does not remove it. But when an individual takes action to remove the headache, the headache is more easily released. It is the intent and the knowing behind the action that assists in removing the headache. Similarly, when you know what actions to take, and set an intention to do so, you are more likely to fulfill your life's purpose.

To successfully fulfill your life's purpose, you need to be clear in understanding what that purpose is and you need to feel your alignment with it. Then you need to be aware of what actions to take to fulfill it and, of course, be willing to actually take the steps and actions. It can be a lifetime of being that brings you into the fulfillment of your life's purpose, or it can be that during the course of your life you continually perform your purpose. To discover your life's purpose, it is important to be in tune with your heart's desire, be aware of what brings you joy and enthusiasm and also be aware of what gifts and talents you have to offer. All too often we get caught up in activities that don't bring us joy. We do what is necessary to bring food to the table but do our activities bring fulfillment to our soul and to our being?

What would it be like to enjoy your life to the fullest? Ask yourself what dreams you have and what brings you great joy? When you examine this, you can better ascertain the underlying reason for it.

For example, if you feel you would live your dream life by offering service to others by way of hospital administration, you could say the underlying fulfillment is being of service to others by improving their health. Perhaps you have the desire to be a homemaker, providing the necessary comfort and basic needs to your children or spouse. The underlying fulfillment is being of service to your family.

In all ways and all functions, you are providing some type of service to others. It is best that you realize the capacity, ability and propensity you have that is indeed there, sometimes waiting to come forth, so you can express the highest form of who you are. When you release this inner expressiveness there is a fulfillment of your life's purpose.

All Our Puzzle Pieces are Necessary

Let us examine more closely just what is really occurring when you honor and allow your truest authentic life's purpose to be expressed. (There can be multiple purposes, by the way.) The expression of The One comes through you when you allow yourself to be the vehicle by which a particular function of the whole is expressed. Recall the firefighter being in the function of providing firefighting services. This person's service is relevant to the whole, but has a small piece of the puzzle to fulfill, while others have other pieces of the puzzle to fulfill. When we put together *all* the pieces of the puzzle (each person fulfilling their purpose and thus providing their puzzle piece) then we get the complete and whole picture. The same is true with the functioning of humanity, which runs smoother when each person is fulfilling their life's function; that is, when *all* the puzzle pieces are put into place. When each of us follows our heart's desire, we are allowing The Creator to express through us. This allows for the further expansion of life, which is necessary for the expansiveness and expression of The Creator Itself.

You can appreciate coming from the "place" of The One when you allow yourself to be grounded and rooted in a place of living authentically. For when you do, you are then truly fulfilling your life's purpose, for you are allowing the expression that is unique to you to come through. And this is essential to bring about The Creator's fulfillment of Itself. Everything each person does is of service, in some form or another. It may be something that requires further refinement to then lead to the final delivery of service.

Exercise

Sit with the concept for a while and assess what you are currently doing that is of service to others. How can you be of better service?

Are you following your heart's desire? If not, why not? Take a piece of paper and examine what it is that you're doing with your life now and ask yourself if this is the expression of you that you feel represents your purpose in life. If you are a college student, you can say your purpose is preparing, through studies, to offer your services once your studies are complete. Examine what is your heart's vision of living your life's purpose. What would it take to live your life's purpose, if not already living it?

Chapter 32
Cumulative Experiences of Your Life

In a manner that is likened to the trees in a forest, you also bring with you your individual form to the planet.

Your purpose here is to fully express the uniqueness of who you are in a manner that lightens and betters all of humanity. Without your light the world would be a different place. Do you better understand the necessity of your gifts and talents, as well as those of all people on earth? When you begin to appreciate the delight of life itself, and when you create the desired outcome of your life, which is to fulfill your life's purpose, then you can be assured you are contributing to the divine intricacies and the whole of all life. When you can appreciate this, then you better appreciate all the other souls on the planet contributing in the same manner.

All Our Experiences are Important Components
You offer the gifts and talents, unique circumstances, and experiences, beliefs, intentions and goals to your own life. When all these elements are put together they form a compilation of what you experience as your life. During the course of your lifetime, you accumulate knowledge and experiences in such a manner that has the cumulative effect of benefiting your being so that you have the tools and consciousness to carry with you into the next stage of your life, to create the outcome of what you're here to accomplish. To illustrate this concept, let us take an example of a woman in her thirties, involved with helping the homeless. In the course of her life she herself had been homeless, which gives her insight into how it feels to be homeless and therefore she is better able to help homeless people become self-sufficient. She has the gifts and talents to help people feel

at ease with her, a gift of listening and being compassionate toward others, being detail-oriented and has a deep wisdom of understanding people's needs.

She uses these gifts and talents as a means to interact with and assist the homeless at the shelter she founded. We can see how she applies her gifts and talents to bringing positive change for her clientele.

She had various accumulated experiences and knowledge that are directly beneficial to her understanding the needs of homeless people and effectively assisting them with receiving self-sufficiency education. As a result of the deep difficulties she experienced she is now able to help other homeless people in a far better capacity because of her accumulated experiences and knowledge.

Exercise

Think about how your life's experiences and knowledge has led you to where you are now and what gifts and talents you share with others. See if you can recognize the positive blessings that have come as a result of your different life's experiences.

Also look at where you might be if you hadn't had the experiences you had. Would you have as deep a knowing and understanding of things if you didn't experience certain events in your life?

What contributions to humanity can be or has been given, as a result of people's experiences? Think of people you know who have made contributions to other people's lives as a result of their own past experiences.

Give yourself praise, show yourself appreciation and recognize you are, always have, and always will be offering your best to helping others, contributing to a project or making a difference in other ways. Recognize you are here as a great representation of The Creator, manifested through you. Uphold yourself in the highest regard.

Chapter 33
Creating Peace Within

Peace within, peace on earth.

When you surrender and relax with life, you are telling The One that you trust. You are telling yourself you are relaxed enough to have what is to occur to come to you, for you know there is only good intent for you, given to you by The One.

Imagine having always been treated with kindness and high regard, being treated in a way that brings you comfort and harmony. When you are treated in this manner then you learn to trust the source from which this treatment came. The same is true when you see that each one of us is treated well by The One, who always provides what we ask for. Therefore, it's important to be aware of your thoughts and be aware of where you focus your thoughts so your needs and desires are met.

Remember the defining moments in your life that brought great success and a sense of accomplishment? Think of what it was that led to those moments. What did you do to accomplish what you set out to accomplish? When you analyze each of these defining moments in your life, you will see that the reason for the accomplishment was how you set your mind to it. You focused clearly and intently on it. You set your intention to accomplish a goal. You focused your time and energy on the tasks required to accomplish what you desired, and in doing so, you set into motion the necessary actions that brought forth your successful outcome. Sometimes the desired outcome came out in a way you expected and sometimes it did not. But always it came in the highest and best form for you and for the others involved. This is where the aspect of trust comes in. When you recognize you are applying yourself in the best way you can (which is almost always the case) and recognize The Creator always provides, then you can be at more peace within yourself. You can avoid having regrets for having done things in a certain way.

Exercise
Contemplate now what the defining moments were in your life that you felt were great accomplishments in which you set your intention on and focused your efforts on. Consider how the event would have turned out if you hadn't applied yourself as you did. Would it have turned out the same? Now consider the aspect of trust discussed above. When do you feel you can trust that you are indeed being provided for? Is it when you see the desired outcome as you expected? When the outcome isn't what you expect do you find yourself distrusting? What is your reaction to it when the outcome isn't what you expected? Do you still trust yourself and/or The One? Do you believe the difficulties presented to you in life are gifts you can learn from and do you embrace them?

When you examine the answers to these questions, you begin to better appreciate your longing to be at peace so you can better relax into your life. You can better understand the reasons that drive you to do what you do in a manner that brings forth the discoveries of yourself in a way that propagates and helps to further your self-development. For is it not the purpose of your life to learn and build upon your experiences so that you can better build your character, your being, so you can better fulfill your purpose in life?

When you are aware of your life's purpose, you can, of course, examine what action steps to take, and set your intention to do so. In doing this, you offer your gifts and talents to the world. It is up to you to bring forth your desires by applying yourself. You do this by choosing what thoughts you have so you intentionally create your desires, and to have the faith and trust that once you have these thoughts and take appropriate action (along with intent), you can more easily see the outcome. All the while, it is important to recognize you must, for it provides the peace you seek, have the deep faith and trust that the best is what occurs for you, even if the outcome is not what you expected. All too often, people think things should turn out in a certain way, only to be surprised when it doesn't. And they wonder why not. But upon a closer examination, the truth is, the person received what they were thinking.

Another important thing to do in order to create peace within yourself is to understand that the timing of your desires is subject to the highest and best good for you, and therefore it is best to trust that The Creator knows when this is. For The Creator has all the pieces to the puzzle and therefore has the full perspective of all life.

Along the same lines, you can see that the outcome of your defining moments involved all the people and circumstances that surrounded those moments. When you examine the circumstances and events that contribute to your defining moments, you must also consider the interconnectivity of the results and actions that occur.

Let us examine a scenario that can better help us understand the interconnectivity that is present in our defining moments. We are going to give the example of a building being built. The construction supervisor has the permit to build a building that is in, what environmentalists consider, a nature preserve. If the building were to be built here, many bird's and animal's homes would be destroyed and they would be dislocated. The construction of this building is vital to the economy of the small town, and the area is such that there is little option to place the building elsewhere. The developer's defining moment would be to receive permission to build this structure, but the citizens have gathered and have formed a protest to stop the construction. When the courts examine the options, it is realized that there is a parcel of land adjacent to the wetlands, and the decision was made to move the building permit to that location. This becomes the defining moment for the developer in that the structure will still be built, and also the defining moment for the citizens and environmentalists for the wetlands will remain untouched. The consideration of all parties allowed for the resolution to have quite a positive outcome. We can see the interconnectivity of life at play here, the necessity of having all aspects considered so nothing would be harmed.

Chapter 34
Why Change is Important

The Creator's nature is to expand and continually express Itself in new ways.

People tend to filter new information to fit it into their existing belief systems. However, there are benefits to bringing in new information so as to expand your existing belief systems into a broader picture, that picture being your life. For when you have new information, you are trying to put the puzzle piece into an existing puzzle, only to find it doesn't fit. The puzzle we're referring to here is your own personal puzzle, your picture of your reality.

When you look at what you're doing in your life in the context of your picture, you are somewhere between being satisfied and at peace with it, or you are dissatisfied, fighting or resisting what is. When you can resolve to accept new things into your life, you are able to create a space in your picture to put the new puzzle piece into. That piece can then contribute to creating a new picture of your life. As you continue to release resistance or negative thoughts, more space within your current picture becomes available for the changes in your life, creating a new landscape. As you experience this expansion and modification of your life, all the while being relaxed and in a surrendered state, you are then more able to create more expansion in your picture, and therefore you begin to see a change in your life. These changes are always good and are meant to help you grow.

Remember, it is the very nature that what is inside needs to come forth and express itself. Just like the seed of a mighty oak cannot do anything but express itself as an oak tree, so it is also true that a human can only express itself as a human. Not only that, but a human needs to express itself with its unique set of gifts, talents and personality traits. Keep in mind that all of life is continually express-ing its innate and divine nature, and that all needs to be there, for all represents the one source, The Creator. When all humans, as well as the plant, animal and mineral kingdoms are expressing, they are all contributing to the whole, and all are necessary components for the successful expression of the one large puzzle that is the picture of all of life.

Trust that Change is Good

Getting back to your own picture, you can begin to appreciate and understand the necessity of your picture to expand and change so that you continue to contribute to the expansiveness of all of life. And when you appreciate and remember the importance of your indi-vidual life to the whole, you can better accept the necessity of allow-ing change into your life. Also, it is easier to allow change when you truly trust it is for the best, even if the change is initially perceived as painful. But when you hold onto the knowing that there is always a gift in each change, you have more peace within yourself regarding the change.

Here is an example of incorporating change into your life. A young man has been an apprentice for several years to be a craftsman and is now ready to move forward into establishing his own business. But he is fearful about setting up a business, so he procrastinates and finds himself in a quandary. He has little income. A change needs to be made. He needs to expand his picture by being willing to incor-porate the piece of the puzzle to include taking responsibility for his own business. Having very little income is an impetus to him taking actions necessary to set up his business, and as a result, his business is now open. He finds business to be slow and, finding this difficult, becomes discouraged. Out of the difficulties and discouragement, he builds fortitude and resolve to devote more focus on creating a suc-cessful business. He is now stronger, more determined and more fo-cused than ever to build a successful business. He has chosen to have positive and focused thoughts and also to believe that his business can be successful. He may not have gotten as motivated and focused if his business had not been slow. He learned he had more strength, fortitude and determination than he realized. Knowing of these strengths is the gift he received as a result of the changes he went through during the transition period between ending his apprenticeship and starting his own business. If his business had taken off quickly, he would not have had the experience of finding out about himself regarding his resilience, determination, motivation, strength and fortitude. Because he learned this about himself, he now knows himself better, and also knows he can tap into these strengths at any time.

When you can trust that all things happen for a reason, and there are gifts you receive in any circumstances in your life, then you can be in a better place of living your life in peace and joy. It is a matter of trusting, being aware, being in tune with your inner guidance (inner wisdom) and also being in a state of surrender and allowance.

Your life will flow easier when you release the oars of your boat. You can better apply your life's knowledge in a way that can precipitate change, or be an impetus to change, in a way that is conducive to bettering your life.

Tragedies Turn to Gifts

There are many examples of how change through tragedy in one's life has turned to an extraordinary (or ordinary) gift to themselves and to others. For example, when the loss of a child causes the grieving mother to create an organization that helps others by bringing awareness and education about drinking and driving, there is the blessing and gift that others receive through this education and awareness. When the gang members kill the son of a prominent attorney, and the attorney, after grieving, creates an organization that provides after-school activities for high school students, there is the gift to help gang members have activities that promote responsible behavior.

So whether the change in a person's life is of a mild or of a tragic nature, the change does lead to expansion. There is the gift of change that promotes the person's ability to further develop their own talents and expand their own life, and in many cases, the lives of others.

Of course, there are some changes that occur without our conscious awareness, or which seem to occur outside of our control. In truth, all changes occur due to our creation, albeit not consciously. It is from our soul level that these changes occur, even those experiences that are considered tragedies.

When you realize you are at choice to relax with the changes in your life, then you can be more at peace with it and thus more relaxed with the flow of your life.

Chapter 35
Bringing Joy and Peace into Your Life

Truly knowing the truth of who you are brings joy and peace to your heart.

If you recognize that when you let your thoughts wonder to nonproductive ways, you can always bring yourself back to better thinking. This is why awareness is so important. Being aware of yourself in how you think and what you think is vital if you are to live a life of joy and peace, for you can more easily bring yourself back to center and connection when you are in observance of yourself. This is called living a conscious life, for it is in the thoughts of your mind that creates your life. So if you want to live with yourself in a more joyful manner then you must have more positive thoughts.

This is easy to say, but how do you go about having pleasant thoughts all or most all of the time? When your boss is being difficult, when your teenager is rebelling, when the rent is due and you don't have the money, when your body aches due to the flu, it is easy to be in a pattern or habit of worrisome, negative, or unhappy thoughts. What can you do to have positive thoughts in the midst of all this? You can start by examining what it is about the situation that causes you to have negative thoughts.

For example, when we are worried about not being able to pay rent, we can see the reason is we spent too much on the groceries and also realize we don't have enough for both. It seems our jobs don't pay enough. We need to relax into the truth and deeply believe we can make more money. We examine our options, such as different employment situations, and all the while, really believe we are able to receive more income. While we are exploring our options, it is essential to be deeply mindful of our approach to this, through our thoughts and also to have *consistent* thoughts of earning more income. Recall the previous discussion of the man seeking a new job, and how his belief that it's difficult to get a new job created a self-fulfilling prophecy. When you deeply believe, and have frequent thoughts of positive results in your endeavors, you will fair better in achieving your desired outcome. An important component in creating your desired outcome is to *feel* the feeling of having that which you desire. Imagine, pretend and make believe, with every fiber of your being, that indeed it is in your life. Recall that your mind does not know the difference between imagining a situation and the real thing. With enough fortitude, tenacity, discipline and deep belief, you can indeed bring to you that which you desire!

What about your worrisome thoughts about your teenager? It is best to be in the place of center and connectivity with The One and live in the present moment. For here, and this is *always* the case, here in the now there is peace and calm. Recognize there is no change to your child's behavior when you worry. It is simply a fact that your thoughts will not change someone else's behavior. You can, however, express your concern with your child, discuss boundaries and behaviors expected from him or her and create natural consequences. But in the end, it is up to you to choose your thoughts, and when you make a mindful attempt to choose positive thoughts, you create a better environment for living with yourself.

Exercise
Try this now. Observe yourself at this very moment. How do you feel? Just stop and ask yourself this question and really be honest with yourself. Are you happy? Are you anxious, sad, or disgruntled? Are you calm and relaxed to finish this book, or in a rush? Simply evaluate and observe yourself in an objective manner, with no judgment if it's good or bad. It just is! Now be aware of your thoughts. What tone are they taking? Are you praising yourself or criticizing yourself? If you are criticizing yourself, what is the topic of the criticism? Who is criticizing

you, the voices of your parents? If you are being pleasant with yourself, what is the topic? Simply be in a place of nonjudgmental observance.

As you go about your day, make a special effort to pay attention and observe how you talk to yourself. Remember the key is that you are aware and are observing yourself. This is a big first step in living a more conscious, joyful and peaceful life.

You can also bring more joy and peace to difficult situations by simply relaxing into them and surrendering to what is. It is often out of your control anyway, so why bring anxiety or angst upon yourself by thinking of it? When your boss is being difficult, and you cannot change his/her behavior (you can never change someone else, you can only change how you react) you can bring more calm within by accepting this is the way he/she is. So, performing in the best manner possible, with integrity and expertise, you can relax in knowing you are safe with keeping your job (if that's what's worrying you). Certainly the circumstances surrounding why your boss is being difficult has some credence on the way you react, but keep in mind you are always at choice as to how you think and what your reaction to the circumstances are.

Hold Yourself in the Highest Glory

Bring yourself peace and joy by being kind, gentle and respectful to yourself and also by having positive and loving thoughts toward yourself. These were previously discussed and it is of such importance that it is beneficial to be reminded of doing this as part of your daily conscious living. Remember you are of the utmost divine nature and deserve to be treated with kindness, love and respect. There is every reason to uphold yourself in the highest glory and esteem. The Creator does, so why not hold yourself in the same high level as The Creator?

Remember to say such words to yourself as: "You are wonderful! You have such love and kindness that you share with others. I love the way you look today! You are always doing your very best and you really are special! Look at your talents and gifts that you share so will-ingly with others! I appreciate you and what you do!"

Know you can talk to yourself at anytime like this and invoke this feeling of self-love and self-appreciation at any time.

It is important to know that even if you don't believe or feel these words are true, say them anyway. In saying them, you will still feel better, and in time you will start believing them. Remember, each of the words here are indeed true about you; you only have to come to the point of believing them to be true for you. It is important to recognize that when you speak this way to yourself, you are not being self-centered or egotistical. The difference between self-loving and self-centered is that self-love recognizes, and comes from the perspective, that all people are of this essence; all people are indeed special. This is because we are all from the same source, The Creator, and each of us have our unique talents and gifts. Everyone is divine. Being self-centered, on the other hand, is when you believe you are better than another person, and that you stand out in a special way that disregards or puts down another, or that doesn't acknowledge the special qualities of another.

So you see here the importance to recognize that self-love comes from the perspective of unity and interconnectivity that all people are special and divine, whereas self-centeredness comes from the perspective of the individual, and that the individual is better than someone else.

You can further bring peace and joy to yourself by recogniz-ing that all events and circumstances in your life occur for a reason. There are no accidents. When you see the gift or lesson you are be-ing given, then you can have peace and joy within. Again, this goes back to if you are willing to explore the lesson you are being given by a difficult situation. In looking at the worrisome circumstances spoken of earlier, how can you bring yourself into more peace and joy? For example, when your boss is being difficult with you, you can ask yourself what lesson is here for you. How are you contributing to this, if anything? What is your boss mirroring to you? What is the gift you can receive from this experience? Or, ask these same questions of your experience with your teenager, or the rent money not being available. What gifts and lessons are here for you to receive and understand? Take a situation in your life now, or from a recent past, that you found yourself being upset, worried, anxious or sad about. Now, as you examine this, see what gift you have received, or could receive from it. Also, see what it would be like to be in the present moment with it, and not resist it, recognizing that as you continue to think the thoughts you've been thinking, it won't change it. Then examine it and see if there's an appropriate action that can be taken.

You will receive great benefit by carefully examining the situation you're evaluating. Take plenty of time to do this. You will learn a great deal about yourself and the benefits of having positive thoughts, and deeply know that all really is well in your life. Also, remember that the soul is orchestrating things for you. "It" knows the whole picture and therefore knows best for your life.

Relaxing, surrendering, and trusting are the best tools to use to create joy and peace inside and knowing that all is well will help you go far in your life.

It is up to you, to choose your thoughts and to decide how best to approach living with yourself. You are at the helm of your own life, taking control of your thoughts and perspective of what it is that you observe in your present state of affairs. When you realize you can bring yourself back to center, live life consciously, and be in a place of self-observance, you can then trust and be more relaxed and at peace.

Chapter 36
Connection with The One and Expansion of Humanity

You are always with The Creator, for you are The Creator expressing your unique way, through your talents, gifts and personality.

In your heart's desire you feel the connection with The Creator. You are always connected, for you and The Creator are one, and it is your goal to feel and be aware of this connection. For to feel this, you are better able to exude the qualities of The One (peace, joy, love, harmony, beauty, creativity, respect, reverence, and kindness). It is the awareness that brings to you the quality that has the natural opportunity to express itself through you when you live your life in tandem with The One. And while the essence is always there, it is your choosing to be aware and choosing to live in a conscious manner that helps encourage and flourish those qualities.

The Right Conditions
Think of a plant with its flowers blossoming in the spring. It is there simply because it needs to express itself. The time to do so is in the spring, and it expands upon itself by exhibiting its flowers. It responds to the right conditions: proper soil, sun and water. These give the plant the right environment to flourish. It is always connected to The One.

In the same way, you too are ever expressing your being and can flourish and grow, given the right material to do so. In your case the right material, the fertile soil of the human, is the awareness and intention you put your mind to. Much is through conscious living, and what helps tremendously in living consciously is the sun, which is analogous to meditation. It is the light of the sun that brings you closer to and encourages you to feel connected and that assists you in living your life in the way it innately needs to live. It is through meditation that provides the fertile soil upon which you flourish. It is the sun that is the ever-continual nourishment that feeds your being in such a way as to feel the connection to The One.

The water that helps feed the plant is another necessary element that allows the plant and its flowers to blossom and flourish. In the same way the water provides this, your mind continually runs through the awareness and consciousness that provides your feelings of connection. This is to say that the sun provides the medium to which we arrive, the meditation provides the medium to feel connected and the awareness provides the continual stream (water) of consciousness to the Divine. The continual flow is required to live more fully and in tandem with The One, in such a way as to provide more serenity, peace, and joy.

It is the surrender to The One that provides for easier navigation through the forest of life and in doing so you are better able to express your authenticity and therefore your true being. In this way the expressiveness of The One occurs, so you can see the interconnectivity of all of life when you look at all the individuals, plants, animals and minerals coming forth in their natural way.

You rest upon the earth in the way that accelerates your learning. You establish the conditions you are living in, in such a way as to express your true nature, given you can be in tandem with The One. All the while, be aware you can also bring forth the qualities of The Creator. Imagine a world in which we are all free to express ourselves authentically, where there is no strife; where all people of the earth are free to be authentic, following their innate being. There would be much joy and peace within, as well as among all people. We can strive to live more authentically and in doing so, be more in flow with life. There would be a better understanding of others to live in their natural way. There would be more reverence for plants, animals and Mother Earth. We would see a rebalancing and new life come forth as a result of the newfound harmony between all people. The kindness and respect, the harmony and joy that would flourish as a result of the fertile soil of all people living authentically would help bring peace to this earth.

The encouragement of repairing the devastation to Mother Earth and its people would be increased. People would come forth with new ways to live so that our impact on using Mother Earth's resources would work in tandem with her, rather than hurt her.

Our children would learn from example the more harmonious ways to interact with others. Children would have a better sense and appreciation of the interconnectivity of life, therefore they would provide for the continuation of the new way of life, that of kindness, respect, joy, peace and harmony.

You can always choose your thoughts, this we know. You can express your divine nature in such a way as to express your true nature, your true essence. You can always live in harmony within yourself when you create from your essence, allowing your self-truths to come forth. You can always live in peace with yourself when you love and appreciate yourself and your uniqueness. You can bestow loving kindness to others and yourself, in the way that it is meant to. Be your own best friend. Be of clear mind and heart to begin each day with the desire to be your very best. You can realize you are showing up authentically when you feel more at ease with yourself and when you feel more empowered. There is a certain light that shines forth from your being when you live your life in this manner.

Heaven on Earth Meditation
We are now going to take a journey of the heart. See yourself in a meadow, the likes of which has never been seen. Visual-

ize and inhale the beauty and wonderful fragrances. Hear the birds singing to one another. Embrace the perfect weather and the clear blue sky. Relax and feel at ease with life. You are in a state of being that is your innermost place of calm and peace. Relax into your heart space and see yourself deepening into your body's relaxed state. Imagine you are floating along in the heavens and you find The One, in front of you, within you, and all around you. You are feeling the deep, immense sensation of utter joy and peace. You are at one with The Creator and The Creator is at one with you. Realizing that you are here with The Creator, you ask, "What is my purpose here on earth"? The One answers, "My child, your purpose here is to provide yourself with the fulfillment of your desires, to express that which desires to come forth. You are here to fully express who you are, with the qualities of you that make you unique." As you listen to these words and know deeply these are words of truth, you realize you have come full circle with your life. You are indeed expressing your unique qualities. You have joy and peace, you show reverence to all of life, and are of great service to humanity, in your own way. There is a sense of fulfillment. And you now know heaven on earth. Breathe this into all areas of your being. Be of the knowing you can experience this place within you at any time, simply by remembering the beautiful meadow you started from.

Now, bring yourself back to where you are sitting and relax. Reflect upon the experience you just had and let it soak into every fiber of your being.

When you know the feeling of what it's like to be at true peace and joy, you can easier invoke this within yourself and live your life more fully.

Chapter 37
Bringing it all Together

The grand understanding of life is ultimately pure joy and peace, pure expression of The One, pure authenticity of our selves, expressing fully the grand glory of The One.

The turmoil, struggle and inner battles that millions have, and continue to have, build an arena that is conducive to war, unrest and disharmony. With this being so wide-spread on the whole planet, how can we ever hope for positive change and ultimately peace?

The true root cause of all discord, all war, and all disharmonies on our planet is due to the separation we humans have from our only important connection to our source, our authentic selves, and to The Creator.

Recall our initial statement at the beginning of this book: We are all one connected. It is through our being that The One exists. The One expresses through each one of us. We are the hands, eyes, ears, heart, and the light of The Creator. We are the individual expression of The Creator that needs to express in an ever-expanding manner. And so, it is vital to bring ourselves back to deeply living in connection with our source, The One, to deeply embrace the knowing, and the living, that we are all that is. We are at a brink of annihilation of the human race. We can and must recognize and live our connection to The One. We must cast aside any notion that we are separate from The One, and cast aside any notion we are separate from others, as well as recognize we are connected to everything; plants, animals, minerals, Mother Earth, the planets, stars, galaxies and beyond.

Kate Heartsong

Recall the discussions presented in Chapter 3 where we looked at the enormity of the variety of life that exists in the universe, the different perspectives there are and the microcosm and the macrocosm.

You Can Choose to Make a Difference
What will it take for you to resolve to find, and then live, your connection to all? What would you like to commit to, in order to bring about much needed change within yourself that will foster joy and peace within yourself? You can then see the results of this manifest in your life. Are you willing to discipline yourself to incorporate on a daily basis the suggestions put forth in this book, such as:

- Be aware of yourself and your impact on others.

- Be in a state of reverence for all life.

- Recognize we are all one connected.

- Appreciate, love and honor yourself. If you aren't quite there, practice exercises to bring up your self-esteem.

- Set an intention for the new day.

- Set an intention for your sleep.

- Be mindful of your thoughts; having positive and loving ones.

- Be kind, gentle and respectful to yourself.

- Write your blessings and accomplishments in a journal.

- Meditate daily or twice daily for at least 15 minutes.

- Remember the enormous expansiveness of the universe, whether this is from a perspective of the stars and galaxies, or your human body and atoms, and its many interconnected functions.

- Be authentic, taking the necessary steps to be this way.

- Practice kindness, love and respect, toward all of life.

- Remember and practice your gifts, talents and personality. Hold them dear to your heart.

- Live from a place of center; that is, be connected to The Creator.

- Get back to center if you get away from there.

- Do special things for yourself to remember the greatness of who you are.

- Be kind to Mother Earth, using her resources wisely and with reverence.

- Visualize and feel your ideal life.

- Remember and invoke special memories of being greatly loved, so you can carry this feeling, this love essence, with you.

- Visit your sanctuary in your meditations.

- Invoke your anchor to bring yourself back to center.

- Live in a state of trust and surrender, knowing all is provided for you by The Creator.

Kate Heartsong

- Remember you're doing the best you can, you always have and you always will.

- Find solace in the fact that you being here is enough evidence that you are important to the whole universe.

Exercise
Sit and reflect on all these suggestions and see which ones you would like to spend more effort on. Do not feel you must master all of these at once. Indeed it is better to experience and work with one or two at a time, then as they become more a part of your life, take on another one or two. During the course of reading this book and having experienced the writings, exercises and meditations offered here, you have had the opportunity to work with and incorporate the material. Now, as you near the end of this journey, find the gifts that these tools offer and slowly and at a pace that feels right for you, resolve and intend to incorporate those tools that best resonate with you. In time, take on another one or two. Remember to be gentle with yourself as you use these tools, knowing deeply you are adapting these into your being for the purpose of being joyful and peaceful, and to also live in the knowing, appreciation and embracing of the interconnectivity of all life. Recall that it is in the knowing, and the living, of the interconnectivity of all life that facilitates your ability to provide the fertile soil of harmony, peace, love and respect for all of life. And when you start with yourself with these, the natural outcome is that these pour out to the world.

Sit in a comfortable chair and contemplate all these words. Relax into the meaning each holds, and examine where you are now, as compared to when you first started with this book.

Now ask:

- What can I do for myself to bring more peace and joy? What can I do to further develop it?

- Where can I make a positive difference for another human being?

- What can I carry with me daily to reinforce my knowing of the interconnectivity of life?

- Where would I like to be a year from now? Five years?

- How can I further express my gifts and talents, so I may be of most benefit to myself and others?

- Is there anything else I'd like to provide that will remind me of my great glory?

- What resistances do I have to embracing the full glory and magnificence of who I am?

- Am I dedicated enough to meditate daily? If not, what is stopping me from this practice?

- Upon further inspection of my moods and emotions, can I expect myself to be happy? How can I be my own best friend? How shall I treat myself?

When you realize you are the light of the world, in all its glory and radiance, when you can rise above your circumstances in total trust that you are provided for always and in all ways, when you realize there is no separation between you and The One, you and others, you and the rest of life, when you can truly embody the knowing that you deserve all good, then you can help promote your relaxed state of being, and help promote more joy and peace for yourself and the planet, and the collective consciousness (the combined consciousness of all people).

Reflect upon your life and bring peace to your heart. Know, despite any difficulties you may experience, all is truly as it should be. We have great gifts in each circumstance and we find the blessings in them. Go now and be well, in the goodness of life. Be of deep peace that you and everyone else are in the place of most authentic joy and peace. In the higher realms of The One, this is the absolute reality! It has already been in existence. Now, bring this into your heart and know it to be your absolute reality. Do this now and fully embrace this gift that has been given to you in this moment of time.

Chapter 38
Creating a Vessel for Receiving

It is as you believe.

When you have a belief inside yourself, you can then see the manifestation or outpicturing of it in your life. Imagine having a song in your mind, you dance and sing. This is the outpicturing of the song that was in your head. When you believe you can receive your heart's desire, you begin to create a receiving vessel within your being. It is as if you can create an opening that allows you to receive. It is as important to believe and know that you can receive your heart's desire as it is to envision your desire itself. You create the conditions needed to accomplish your life's purpose by knowing yourself well and honoring your inner guidance. Also, you are more in alignment with The One when you are in a place of authenticity, that is, when you are following your heart's desire and your life's purpose.

Suppose, for example, you desire to bring required funds to support a project that provides clothing to needy children worldwide. When you are in a place of authenticity, when you set your intention and desire to fulfill your life's purpose, when you truly believe and know this is possible and when you trust and surrender to The One, you have a much better chance of receiving the funds for those needy children.

Be in alignment with your heart's desire and know you can and will receive it. When you believe, you see the manifestation come forth. It is as if the stirring of the cosmic juices conglomerate and gather into the desired outcome and go to a vessel that is available for docking the outcome. The important point here is to *allow* your-self to receive what you desire. Cast aside any thought of doubt and release all worries or concerns as to when and how your heart's desire will come to fruition.

Creating the vessel does entail trust and faith in The Creator. You can well imagine the first requirement is to release fear and sim-ply know all is being divinely guided and orchestrated for your well-being. The soul knows best what to create and bring forth to you. You are one and the same and, yes, you have free will, and yet there is the undercurrent, the ever flowing river of life that is there, and you're life is being navigated. You can realize there are elements that are put into place for the necessary conditions that then provide you the tools to learn and grow. You can put these into place for the best conditions to come forth. When you then grow and expand due to these customized life conditions, you are better able to live in tandem with The One, and therefore are fulfilling your life's purpose.

Suppose you came across a river that is too wide to cross, you would try to figure out what other options there are for you. You could try to swim but the current is too wild. You could find a boat to carry you but this would require backtracking. You could go around the river, but this would take days. You could find a place along the river that narrows, that provides the same course of action, that of crossing the river, and you have found the area that makes it viable: the place where the river is narrow enough for you to accomplish your desire (to cross the river). In your accomplishment, you realize you have come to your destination and you relax. When you are trusting that your heart's desires will be provided for you, it is easier to know you will indeed find the way to cross the river, even though there may be difficulties to overcome. Remember that when you are presented with what you perceive to be difficulties in life, you learn and grow from them. You become more complete in your endeavors to accom-plish your purpose in life.

Chapter 39
Be an Ambassador

It is in the very nature of The Creator to have perfection in everything.

All is in divine right order and so it shall always be. It cannot be otherwise. It is from the human mind that we recognize from our perspective what we know as our reality. Remember it is a limited perspective because we are limited to the five senses, which is required to live in the physical world. Our interaction with our surroundings is such that we perceive with our five senses (six for some, the sixth being intuition or inner wisdom). It is by design that we experience and interact in this physicality, so we may experience the very essence of life in this modality.

Through our emotions and feelings, we also interact. It is through our various experiences with others, and the environment, that we get to know who we are. And in getting to know who we are, we then are better able to create our own reality, for when we can better understand and know ourselves, we can then better project out what we desire to change or desire to bring into our lives.

The Role of an Ambassador

Imagine if you became the ambassador to a foreign country. You would become a negotiator. How does this occur when you interact with others? To know yourself allows you to be adept at interacting with others in a manner that provides a positive outcome. This is a necessary skill and gift in negotiating and in being an ambassador. When you interact in this manner with all people in all interactions, you can accomplish positive outcomes on the planet. You are using your experience and skills to bring forth the desired outcome, which is the resolution to the particular conflict or situation at hand.

Kate Heartsong

When you look at this from the perspective of your view point, you see only a limited view. You use your skills you have from your physicality stand point. The ambassador uses his/her six senses and this facilitates the process well. But there is another factor, that being of The One perspective; it recognizes the delight of the process and the interaction and interconnectivity of all people involved in the negotiation. There is a synergistic effect that occurs as a result of the interaction between the two parties. And it is in this synergy, the creation of a third element, which brings about the momentum of the negotiations. So you see, there are not only the six senses being used, but the third element that arises as a result of the interaction.

Recognize that the leveling of the beliefs you hold toward one another will be of great benefit to all of humanity. When you approach others in the similar manner as the ambassador, you are more able to create an environment of neutrality and harmony, peace and respect. Remember, when you create an atmosphere of congeniality, you foster harmony and understanding. You create an opening for thriving and encouraging goodwill between the two parties. The synergy that is created helps to further foster that goodwill. This third force of synergy enables the betterment of all of humanity, for since we are one connected, all is affected by the interaction of the two ambassadors in negotiation. Or in the case of any other people interacting, the same situation occurs: there is synergy, and this affects all people on the earth.

Imagine then, the cumulative effect of all the people's interactions with each other (whether it is verbal or nonverbal). There is much residue of the impact of the positive and of the negative interactions. The collective consciousness of all people is such to have in its womb the chaos, war, hate, misunderstandings, negativity, as well as love, compassion, hope, kindness, and respect. When it is dissected and analyzed, you can have what you perceive to be good elements, at least, that which you perceive to be good. In the ultimate reality there is no difference between good and bad. But in your mode of living in physicality, you have created the distinction between these two in order for you to discern and to experience yourself to the fullest. And that is to know yourself, for The One's very nature is to know Itself.

When you separate out the elements of good and bad and see its wisdom and gifts, then you are better able to understand the wide variety of options available to you. You can choose to be of good spirit and kindness to others, and open your hearts to create and nourish an environment that is conducive to a loving atmosphere. Or you can choose to interact with another in a way that fosters disrespect and negative or ill feelings. But what you do to another, you do to yourself. For what you put out comes back to you. What is inside of you is manifested in what you see as your reality. Consider this concept with the fact that we're all one connected. It is much better, of course, to foster a pleasant environment, one that offers respect, love, nonjudgmental acceptance of what is, support and kindness, for we feel better when we're in this arena. It feels better to see others in this arena as well.

So why not create this environment for your life and the life of others? Be an "ambassador" in each encounter and interaction with another, whether that is a person, plant, animal, mineral, or Mother Earth. See and feel with the eyes and heart of love, compassion, respect, acceptance, kindness, and understanding when you are in any type of interaction. And remember to do the same with the interactions with yourself since it feels better to be in a place of love and respect with yourself as well.

Imagine the synergy that's created from this throughout the planet and throughout the universe.

Exercise
Sit with this concept for a while and set an intention to approach your day in this manner. Bring yourself to a place of center and then open your heart. As you go about your day, remember the interconnectivity of all of life by telling yourself as you see a person, that you are connected with that person. Be from a

place of respect, love and kindness just for today. See what kind of day you have. Be aware of how you talk to yourself. If you are critical, change your tone and say kind things.

Continue to do this for another day. And then another. Continue practicing this. Be gentle and kind to yourself. Simply remind yourself you are magnificent and are the glory of The One. Discipline yourself to be living your life this way as much as possible. Soon, it can become a way of life, if you so choose. You always have a choice.

In your journal, write down at the end of the day your experiences and observations of how your day went. Was it different than before? If so, how? And observe how you feel inside. Do you feel more at peace? If not, you will, with continued practice, and sincere intent. Be an observer of yourself and watch the positive possibilities grow.

The positive impact you make is felt not only by you but by many others around you and around the globe.

Chapter 40
We Are All One

It is our right to live a life of ease and grace.

All the separation from The Creator has caused discord with our-selves and this has been and continues to be manifested on what we currently see as the world affairs.

Imagine what it feels like to be in harmony within yourself, and how this would be manifested in the world. Imagine a life of con-tinual flow, gliding on the river of life in the way you were meant to: with joy, peace and harmony. Imagine the heaven on earth that would reside within you. Yes, you may have challenging times in your life, for without them, you would not grow, but imagine living a life of true connection, through and through, with The One. Imagine the sweetness of life, the deep and vast grace of The One, in which you absolutely live in; where you are thoroughly and deeply saturated in the love of The One. You are always saturated with The One's love and grace, peace and harmony; however, it is the conditioning that you have that has put the cover on, covering up and limiting your ac-cess to living in your true modality.

Your journey in this lifetime and many lifetimes is to dismantle your conditioning and to more easily access the true essence and the true nature of your being. Here, where heaven resides in your heart, you feel the true peace and calm that has been with you all along. It is within this realm of light and of love, that you better access your true nature, the Divine, your true light. When given the opportunity to live from this place of center and connection, this place that allows you to be authentic, this place of The One, pure Spirit, you can bet-ter express yourself and your light shines all the brighter. Imagine a world where all people are given the same opportunity to shine their light brightly, where there is enough food, shelter, safety, love and human connection.

Now imagine when just one person chooses to live in their place of authenticity, and this passes on to another and another. Many more bright lights are lit, until the whole planet reaches the point of light, encompassing The One.

You can bring into your perspective what feels plausible and attainable and that is to *create this for yourself*. Choose to live your life in this place of authenticity, of joy and of peace within. Choose your own thoughts, be aware of your own emotions, body, effects on others; you can choose to be of service to others using your own gifts and talents, you can choose to be kind and gentle with yourself, and with each person you encounter, you can choose to navigate through your life with surrender and trust in The One, knowing you're always provided for. It is up to you to choose.

You may reflect upon all the different concepts presented here in this book, and see what you would like to incorporate into your life, so as to create a new lifestyle for yourself. In doing so, you are creating fertile soil in which joy and peace, love and kindness can grow better. It is a choice you can make for yourself each day, upon awakening by renewing your vows for your life, so you may remind yourself of what is really important.

Being ever-connected to The Creator will always provide the means by which you enjoy your life in the manner it has always been meant to live. Life is easier when the main connector is in place. The main connector being The One. For when you are plugged in, you have the juice, the current of life. This current of life, the forever flowing energies of The One, continually nourishes you and continually provides for your life.

It is in the oneness of all life that you can better appreciate and know the true meaning of all, which is by being you, you who is ever-expressing and ever-expanding, so that The One can experience Itself. You are that which experiences and interconnects with yourself in the way that provides for the expression to flow forth, continually, forever, into infinity.

Bring forth from your heart the joy and peace that is rightfully yours, sharing your light with yourself and others, to a point where the illumination is so bright that all peoples' lights shine in the same manner, so as to exhibit only the great illumination, where all are blended together. The result looks like one big sun, melded together where one person cannot be distinguished from another, forming the One, like the sun, so brilliant and bright. Feel the love, the peace, the joy, the harmony, the beauty of The One—You!

Appendix A Personality Traits

The following is a partial list of personality traits. Carefully and with honesty, review this list for your traits.

Keep in mind there are personality traits that are opposite of some listed here. Examples are: patient and impatient, reliable and unreliable, flexible and inflexible.

adventurous	driven	leader	resourceful
affectionate	egalitarian	logical	respectful
aloof	empathetic	loving	responsible
altruistic	encouraging	loyal	secure
analytical	energetic	mature	self-directed
arrogant	enthusiastic	methodical	selfless
articulate	entrepreneurial	modest	self-starter
assertive	expressive	motivated	self-centered
aware	fair	negative	sensitive
candid	fastidious	nervous	sensual
careful	finicky	nice	serious
caring	flexable	noble	shrewd
charming	focused	nurturing	sincere
clean	forgiving	objective	socially conscious
clever	friendly	open-minded	sober
compassionate	fun	optimistic	spiritual
competitive	generous	organized	stoic
complainer	gentile	over-bearing	strong
confident	good	passionate	subtle
controlling	grateful	passive	sweet
conscious	gregareous	patient	tenacious
considerate	hard-working	perceptive	thorough
cooperative	helpful	pessimistic	timid
courageous	honest	picky	tolerant
courteous	humble	poised	trusting
critical	humerous	polite	trustworthy
curious	independent	practical	unpretentious
decisive	influential	professional	vain
demanding	innovative	proud	visionary
dependable	inspiring	reliable	
detail-oriented	intelligent	realistic	
determined	intuitive	rebellious	
direct	kind	receptive	
disciplined	lazy	relaxed	

Glossary

Altar—A physical place (such as a table) holding special keepsake items. The altar is designated to assist in contemplation, meditation, relaxation, creating sacred space or to invoke feeling calm and peaceful.

Anchor—A stimulus or reminder that, when you think of it, will bring on the feeling that was associated with it when creating the anchor itself.

Aura - The universal life force energy that is connected and unique to each person. All life forms have an aura.

Centering – Bringing yourself into the place of *feeling* connected to The One by gently focusing within yourself, usually focusing in the heart space.

Collective consciousness – The consciousness of all people on the planet added together as one.

Consciousness vantage point – The perspective from which you see something.

Defining moments – Experiences that cause a change or shift in direction of your life.

Ether – The unseen energy that interconnects everything. The all-pervading essence of all that is.

Field of potentiality – All that is in the unmanifested form; that is, that which has not yet manifested into a physical form.

Higher self – The soul. That part of you that gives you inner guidance; also known as gut feelings or intuition.

Manifested form – That which is physically here; already created.

Mirror – An analogy used to describe a phenomena of seeing outside of ourselves what is inside of us. Also known as outpicturing.

Outpicture – That which is within us gets projected to the outside of us. Also known as mirroring.

Sanctuary – An imaginary place a person can create for the purpose of feeling utmost comfort, peace, joy, and harmony. This place is invoked at anytime you desire and is commonly incorporated into a meditation.

Shadow Side – Those aspects of a person that are underneath, not on the forefront, of a person's collection of personality traits, yet may sometimes have an influence of what may be perceived as negative or undesirable.

Soul – That part of you that is the connector or bridge to The Creator. It guides and directs you toward that which is for your highest and best good. Also known as inner guidance, gut feeling, or intuition.

Unmanifested form – That which is not yet created into physical form. It is the field of potentiality.

Universal life force energy – The essence or energy that gives life to the living organism. Also known as chi.

Veil – A metaphor describing the separation from The One that we perceive ourselves as having; a barrier between the reality as we perceive it and the absolute reality of The One.

About the Author

Kate Heartsong is one of today's newest and best-loved international authors. She is also a gifted speaker and her new book entitled *Deeply We Are One* is an extremely engaging and thought-provoking work that leads the way to the 21st century New Thought arena. She has faced and overcome some of life's greatest challenges to become the amazing success she is today both personally and professionally.

Kate holds a BS in Business Administration from Columbia College and also a BA in Psychology from the University of Colorado, which she has used in combination with her dynamic life experiences, deep understanding and intuition to empower individuals in knowing their own unique inner worth and value while assisting them in becoming the highest and best version of themselves.

Her parents, an Austrian father and German mother, escaped wartime Nazi Germany to move to South Africa where she was born. The family then moved to Denver, Colorado when she was 8 months old where she has loved living ever since. Kate became a naturalized citizen of the U.S. because of her love and gratitude for this country. Her own personal journey of self-discovery and transformation began 11 years ago when she found her own inner voice and began writing inspired works to positively impact and change people's lives.

Kate has the heart of a true humanitarian and consistently supports the organizations she is passionate about such as Project Pave, Imagine Peace Foundation, Children's Global Peace Project, Dances of Universal Peace, Heifer International and the Second Wind Foundation. She has been instrumental in helping these organizations reach their goals of supporting people in their local, national and international communities.

Kate is a true visionary leader. She continues to promote peace on earth by empowering others to create peace within themselves. For it is her knowing that the possibility of peace is more real when we start with one person at a time. Kate's own inspirational quote says it best, "Peace Within, Peace on Earth."

DONATIONS MADE FROM SALE PROCEEDS OF

DEEPLY WE ARE ONE

For each book sold, a 10% donation will be made to three of my favorite nonprofit organizations, which may include:

Heifer International

Children's Global Peace Project

Dances of Universal Peace

Project Pave

Second Wind

TO ORDER ADDITIONAL BOOKS

Additional copies of *Deeply We Are One* can be purchased through the author's website:

www.joyfulradiance.com

Also available on www.Amazon.com

www.ingramcontent.com/pod-product-compliance
Lightning Source LLC
LaVergne TN
LVHW011230080426
835509LV00005B/420